Treasures From Above
Eternal Perspectives

Daily Christian Devotionals that Inspire Faith
Includes Biblical Devotional Poetry

By Kenneth L. Birks

~

Published by Straight Arrow Publications
Five-Year Anniversary Revised Edition Updated 2025
www.straitarrow.net
Copyright 2020

Cover Design by Hans Bennewitz
design/illustration/art direction
hans@modedesign.us
www.hansbennewitz.com

Unless otherwise indicated, all Scripture quotations are taken from The Holy Bible, New King James Version

*From heaven above, we catch glimpses of His great treasures.
From the Father's generosity, riches pour in good measures.
More valuable than gold, silver, or rubies, He desires to bless.
Like looking for buried treasure, we uncover, seeking Him above.
From the Father's great storehouse, we're made rich in His love.*

~

My goal is that you may be encouraged in heart and united in love so that you may have the full riches of complete understanding, so that you may know the mystery of God, namely, Christ, in whom are hidden all the treasures of wisdom and knowledge.

Colossians 2:2-3

Foreword

by Doug Hartline

I sometimes find it hard to believe that I have known Ken Birks for two-thirds of my life. Our friendship started when I was a graduate student, and I am now retired. In those forty years, one goes through several phases of life, and in all that time, Ken has always been unwavering in his faith and love of God.

Ken was my pastor for several of these years before God called him into other aspects of ministry, not the least of which is being a Christian author. While serving as Senior Pastor of Golden Valley Christian Center, Ken ensured his congregation was filled with God's Word. Week after week, he demonstrated an in-depth knowledge of God's Word that few will ever attain. I suspect this knowledge now enables his words to flow freely from his pen.

Clearly, a teacher as much as a pastor, Ken illuminated God's Word through logical and contextual interpretations – a very left-sided aspect of one's brain. However, over the years, Ken began demonstrating that he could logically interpret scriptures and possessed a unique gift of poetry that could bring out their beauty. Rare indeed is the man who can so astutely master and utilize both the logical and the creative sides of his brain for the benefit of those he serves.

After reviewing his body of work, Henry Fonda, a famous actor from Hollywood's golden era, once said of his equally renowned friend Jimmy Stewart, *"Just how and when did you get so gosh darn good?"* As I read Ken's latest work, I had those same thoughts. In this new devotional, Ken has transformed from an excellent writer to an exceptional one.

When reading a devotional, one must ask oneself two questions: Is it relevant, and what distinguishes it from the myriad devotionals one can choose from? From my perspective, devotionals can be vital

Foreword – Treasurers from Above

tools to improve our quiet time experience with God. They should be able to bring scriptural insight to us. Scripture is far more important than the words of even the most famous of authors, for it is Scripture that penetrates our souls with God's wisdom and daily guidance. Ken's work herein ensures that God's Word takes center stage and holds its most important place within it to remain timeless and relevant.

However, the remarkable poetry makes this book unique. Poetry can shine a light on God's Word from a different angle in a way that helps us look at it much deeper and often more profoundly. It gives us a unique ability to understand and appreciate God's Word in ways we may never have thought of before. We are suddenly confronted with beauty and clarity in our perceptions of our world and God's Kingdom.

Ben Franklin once said, *"You should write something worth reading or do something worth writing."* While one could say Ken has done both in his ministry, I can, without hesitation, say that he has definitely written something worth reading here. So, I invite you to enter *"Treasures from Above"* – let Ken's ability to paint with words reveal the treasures of the Word of God to you in colors you may never have perceived before.

Thank you, Ken; your book is a true gift to the Body of Christ.

Doug Hartline – *Information Technology Director, The University of California, Retired*

Treasures From Above
By Kenneth L. Birks

Table of Contents

Treasures From Above	1	Renewing of Our Minds	95
The Father's Way	5	Fragrance of the Lord	99
Waiting on the Lord	9	Truth and Error	103
In Sync with God's Purposes	13	Flames of Fire	107
Delighting in God's Love	17	The Potter's Wheel	111
Communicating Your Faith	21	God's Playbook	115
Clearing the Way Forward	25	Great Lovers of God	119
Shifting Shadows of Time	29	Come Holy Spirit	125
Dining with Jesus	33	Stop and Listen!	131
Fulfilling God's Purposes	37	Our Eternal Home	135
The Goodness of God	41	The Suffering Messiah	139
Majesty of Knowing God	45	Standing Firm in Storms	143
Spiritual Authority	49	Embracing Your Future	147
Embracing Transformation	53	Grace Unlimited	151
Embracing the Peace of God	59	Changing Perspectives	155
Breakthrough to the Invisible	63	The Fear of God	159
The Wonders of His Grace	67	Trusting in God Alone	163
Making the Most of Life	71		
The Kingdom Powered Life	75	About the Author	167
The Snares of the Enemy	79	Books & Workbooks	168
Abiding in His Presence	83	Reviews	171
Destiny and Purpose	87	Online Connections	173
Sowing Seeds of Faith	91		

Day 1
Treasures From Above

***Proverbs 3:13-15** Happy is the man who finds wisdom, and the man who gains understanding; ^{14} for her proceeds are better than the profits of silver, and her gain than fine gold. ^{15} She is more precious than rubies, and all the things you desire cannot compare to her.*

Many spend their whole lives looking for lost treasures, only to come up empty. Yet, searching for hidden treasure is a God-given desire that lies in most of us. One of my granddaughter's favorite games to play with me is looking for buried treasure. It shows that something in us delights in looking for buried treasure even at a young age. The remarkable thing is we have all the treasures we could ever ask for at our disposal. All we have to do is look to the heavens above with a seeking heart.

***Proverbs 2:1-6** My Son, if you receive my words, and treasure my commands within you, ^{2} so that you incline your ear to wisdom, and apply your heart to understanding; ^{3} yes, if you cry out for discernment, and lift up your voice for understanding, ^{4} if you seek her as silver, and search for her as hidden treasures; ^{5} then you will understand the fear of the Lord, and find the knowledge of God. ^{6} For the Lord gives wisdom, and from His mouth come knowledge and understanding.*

As we give ourselves to the study of God's word while focusing on what is above rather than earthly pleasures, we discover His word is a treasure map to all the wonderful treasures He has in store for us. As we dig deep into His Word and the revelation of who He is, we discover hidden gems that are much more valuable than gold, silver, rubies, or sapphire. Moreover, the gemstones we discover from His treasure house are eternal and lasting.

As seen from the above Scripture, the fear of God is the key to unlocking these treasures once found. When we embrace the fear of

God, we gain an understanding of all He possesses. Therefore, we should seek it with all our hearts. Writing to the church at Colosse, Paul encouraged them to attain the riches of the full assurance of understanding, to the knowledge of the mystery of God, both Father, and Christ, in whom are hidden all the treasures of wisdom and knowledge. We will never know what treasures await us until we seek the Lord with the same enthusiasm as looking for earthen treasures.

As we seek God to walk on the path He has laid before us, He brings people into our lives with hidden gems. These are often the gems that hold the keys to further unlocking our destiny and purpose. Sometimes, these people are not the people we would typically associate with. But God sees something in them we do not understand. Therefore, He considers them hidden gems until discovered through a bond of fellowship.

We have much to discover as we give ourselves to the mysteries of His word and Spirit. Let us go forth with hearts captivated by the discovery of all that the Holy Spirit desires to reveal in us as He searches out the heart of the Father.

Prayer

Heavenly Father, I lift my heart with a desire to know You and Your word in a way that helps me comprehend the great treasures that await me. Help me to value what's eternal more than what is temporal. Help me dig deep into Your Word so that I may know You more intimately. Teach me to fear Your great name so that I will have a greater understanding of Your eternal love that flows freely from Your magnificent treasure chest.

Poem: Treasures From Above

From heaven above, we glimpse His great treasures.
In generosity, Father God pours riches in good measures.
More valuable than gold, silver, or rubies, He blesses.
Like buried treasure, we uncover, seeking Him above.
From His great storehouse, He makes rich in His love.

Treasurers from Above

His word a treasure map, He no longer conceals.
Given to the study of His word, we unseal.
Gaining insight, we delight in revelation from above.
Treasuring His commands with wisdom, we probe.
Revelation embraced, greater knowledge enrobes.

Gems discovered in fearing God, endeavors elevate.
The key found, locked treasurers exposed, we renovate.
Fearing Him, greater insight is gained into treasures.
Sensing value increasing, we dig deeper into who He is.
Gold, silver, rubies, sapphires contrasting, we dig deeper.

Looking for gems, our need for others, we discover.
Treasures in earthen vessels filled, we esteem others.
Drawing from others in humility, gems we uncover.
Knitted in love, we attain all riches in full assurance.
Commanded to love, treasures come in abundance.

Enlightened, we gaze into the Father's treasure chest.
Awakened to the Spirit, He reveals the Father's best.
Revealing treasures as needed, He discloses to fulfill.
Wisdom and revelation revealed, inheritance increases.
Given freely to His Spirit, treasures continually unleash.

In all revealed, we delight in treasures declared.
Given to what's not seen, we aim for what's prepared.
Until then and beyond, treasures flow freely in abundance.
Abundance of treasures revealed, His Word vindicates.
Throughout eternity, His treasures remain never-ending.

Scriptures to Meditate Upon

Job 28:12-28, 2 Corinthians 4:7, Proverbs 2:1-6, Colossians 2:2-3, 1 Corinthians 2:9-10 Proverbs: 3:13-15, Ephesians 1:17-18.

~

May God bless you richly today as you seek to find all hidden away for your discovery.

Day 2
The Father's Way

John 14:2-4 *"In My Father's house are many mansions (dwellings). If it were not for this, I would have told you. I go to prepare a place for you. ³ And if I go and prepare a place for you, I will come again and receive you to Myself, that where I am, there you may be also. ⁴ And where I go, you know, and the way you know."*

Many roads lead to spirituality, but only one way leads to the Father above, who shows the way to the eternal home His Son, Jesus, is preparing for us.

Whether we know Christ as our Lord and Savior or not, we are all spiritual beings with an inherent spirituality. Satan, himself, is a spiritual being. He was one of the highest archangels closest to the Father. The question is, whose voice are you following? There are many voices of spirituality clamoring for our attention, but only one voice will lead us to the Father's way.

Jesus said, *"I am the way, the truth, and the life. No one comes to the Father except through Me."* He also said, *"My sheep hear My voice, and I know them, and they follow me."*

When Jesus spoke to the Pharisees, who had lost their way, He said, *"You are of your father, the devil, who speaks lies from his own resources, for he is a liar and the father of it."*

Let us not be like the Pharisees who lost their way and fell into the devil's ploys. Instead, let us be like sheep who consistently hear their Master's voice. To continually listen to the voice of our Shepherd requires a humble and contrite heart. Otherwise, we open ourselves up to the many deceiving voices from the father of lies.

Isaiah 66:2 "For all these things My hand has made, and all those things exist," Says the Lord. "But on this one will I look: On Him who is poor and of a contrite spirit, and who trembles at My word."

The Father's Way – Treasurers from Above

Two things mentioned in the passage above are necessary to find and remain on the Father's way. The first is having a humble and contrite heart. The second is having incredible respect and love for His Word, which causes us to tremble.

Knowing the Father's thoughts and ways are much higher than ours; our part is to submit to the Father of spirits and live humbly. We are to humble ourselves in His presence by dying to pride and ego. In doing so, we open our hearts to hear the voice of the Shepherd as He speaks words of comfort while showing the way to His excellent treasure house in the heavens above.

The Father's way demands that we embrace the cross of Christ and all that it entails. At the entrance to the path leading to the Father's eternal home, a cross must be picked up and carried before entry is allowed. As the apostle Paul said, this is something we do daily. We must now lose ourselves in Christ by embracing the cross.

Matthew 16:24-25 *Then Jesus said to His disciples, "If anyone desires to come after Me, let him deny himself, and take up his cross, and follow Me. [25] For whosoever desires to save his life will lose it. But whoever loses his life for my sake will find it."*

As we esteem His word more than our necessary food in the same way that Job did, we hold fast to the path that leads to our eternal home.[1] The Father's way is continually made clear by trembling and clinging to His word. As His word becomes a lamp unto our feet, He brightens our path. With His path illuminated, we are not led astray by the many voices within our cultures continually clamoring and competing for our attention. We must be like David, who rejoiced in His word, knowing it would lead to great treasures.

Psalm 119:162 *I rejoice at Your word as one who finds great treasure.*

Prayer

Father God, I come to You in humility, asking You to keep me on the path that leads to the eternal home. Help me to stay humble and contrite in all that I do. Keep me as the apple of Your eye.

---

[1] Job 23:12

Poem: One Way to Heaven Above

Father God, the creator of all, provides a way.
Many roads touted, many miss the way.
Any old road will get you there, they say.
A narrow path to the Father, few find the way.
Blinded, many turn to the devil's highway.

Father's way drawing, Jesus, the only way in sight.
Discovering His way, we come, humble and contrite.
Clinging to Him, pride destroyed, the path is bright.
Blinded by desires, the prideful can't see from distance.
Unable to be drawn, they stand foolishly in resistance.

Mediating between man and God, Jesus makes way.
God in flesh, He ransoms those who believe and pray.
Without sin, made sinful, He makes them righteous.
With blood shed, the way to the Father is cleared.
Atonement made, the perfect Lamb was slaughtered.

Life of the flesh in the blood, atonement had to be blood.
Scripture says, "There's no remission without bloodshed."
Perfect sacrifice completed; the Father's way is paved.
The way blazed, the Son is given for all to be saved.
Sacrifice not received and believed, many are deceived.

To all coming, the way is made available through His Son.
Jesus, the only way to Heaven above is available to all.
Coming, we follow, embracing His cross wholeheartedly.
Cleansed from sin and condemnation, the way clears for entry.
As Author of salvation, all who obey pass by the sentry.

Scriptures to Meditate Upon

John 14:6, Ezekiel 28:12-19, Isaiah 14:12-15, John 8:44, 10:27-28, Hebrews 12:9, James 4:6-10, 1 Corinthians 15:31, Job 23:11-12, Leviticus 17:11.

~

May God bless you richly as you hold firmly to the path that leads to your eternal home filled with treasures beyond comprehension.

Day 3
Waiting on the Lord
It's Implications

Isaiah 40:31 *But those who wait on the Lord shall renew their strength; they shall mount up with wings like eagles, they shall run and not be weary, they shall walk and not faint.*

Do we understand the term "Waiting on the Lord?" In the passage from the book of Isaiah, the prophet gives us a tremendous promise when we learn what it means to wait on the Lord. Do you need your strength renewed? Do you often get weary in well-doing? Do you desire to soar in the spirit? These promises await you as you learn what it means to wait on the Lord.

To wait on the Lord involves prayer, but it is much more than offering up our petitions before God. It is as much or more about listening to Him with a prayerful spirit. In Scripture, we are encouraged to acknowledge God in all our ways, which involves keeping our minds focused on the Lord throughout the day. By acknowledging God in all our practices, we find ourselves praying without ceasing. We must continually lean upon Him in all things.

Proverbs 3:5-6 *Trust in the Lord with all your heart and lean not on your own understanding. In all your ways, acknowledge Him, and He shall direct your paths.*

When we offer Him even the most menial tasks by acknowledging Him in everything we do, we are more in tune to hear Him as He speaks into our spirits as we fulfill our daily tasks. When we do this with our hearts fully engaged and energized, He causes us to run the race without getting weary.

We tend to get so bogged down with the daily minutia that we forget the Holy Spirit is there as our Helper. Jesus relied entirely on the Holy Spirit and His communication with the Father, even during intense ministry times. He did not allow the tyranny of the moment to steal from Him what the Father's purpose was. We see this during one of His ministry times in Capernaum, where He had just healed Peter's mother-in-law, followed by an extensive ministry time of casting out demons and healing many sick with various diseases. The whole city had gathered at the door. Following this anointed time, Jesus slipped out to pray and be alone with His Heavenly Father.

The disciples, wondering where Jesus had disappeared to, went looking for Him the following day because everyone wanted Him to continue to heal and deliver.

When the disciples found Jesus, they said, *"Everyone is looking for you."*

Jesus responded, *"Let us go to the next towns, and I may preach there also because for this purpose, I have come forth."*

After spending time praying and communicating with His Father, Jesus' spirit was refreshed, and His vision and purpose were renewed.

In the same way, Jesus was renewed in vision and purpose, the Holy Spirit desires to renew our vision and purpose each day as we spend time waiting in His presence. As we are faithful to wait on the Lord, He will fill us with insight and purpose as we continually acknowledge and commit all our ways unto Him. He desires to breathe upon us as He renews and strengthens us daily.

Prayer

Lord, I pray that You fill my mind and spirit with Your wisdom and knowledge of who You are. Fill my heart with Your desires towards me so that I may have the mind of Christ as I go about my day. Open the eyes of my understanding and enlighten me to know the hope of Your calling. Help me understand the exceeding greatness of Your power as I commit my day unto You. Renew my strength and cause me to soar like the eagles as I wait upon You.

Poem: Waiting on the Lord

Waiting on the Lord, we keep lamps fully lit.
With strength and vitality, we press to outwit.
Into realms unknown, we go, entirely abandoned.
Given ride on wings of an eagle, we don't faint.
Spirit led, we're free to soar without constraint.

With expectation, we embrace all that's decreed.
The Father's heart searched, He reveals what's needed.
Divine nature imparted, life's perspectives change.
Waiting on the Lord, He freely pours into our hearts.
Divine nature revealing, greatness is known in all parts.

Believing and confessing, faith arises with expectations.
Acknowledging God in all ways, He directs aspirations.
Waiting, fully convinced of His promises, He performs.
Trusting and waiting, He brings to pass hidden desires.
In submission, we embrace all that He requires.

Listening and waiting, He instructs, giving ear to His voice.
Presenting prayers and petitions, He listens and conducts.
Praying without ceasing, our hearts and minds stay on Him.
With a still, small voice, He whispers, giving ear to secrets.
Obediently responding, from faith to faith, we go as zealots.

Waiting patiently, gifts arrive for serving and ministry.
Attentive to the needs of others, we wait in symmetry.
Selfish ambitions set aside, we minister accordingly.
In serving and waiting, grace flows in new dimensions.
Soaring to new heights, we wait on Him, who strengthens.

Scriptures to Meditate Upon

Isaiah 40:31, 1 Corinthians 2-9-11, Mark 1:35-39, Proverbs 29:18, Romans 8:14, 2 Peter 1:2-3, Romans 4:20-22.

~

May God's most precious blessing be upon you as you learn to soar like eagles. May He increase you daily as you give an ear to His voice.

Day 4
In Sync with God's Purposes

Jeremiah 29:11 *For I know the thoughts that I think toward you says the Lord, thoughts of peace and not of evil, to give you a future and a hope.*

The Psalmist David wrote, *"We are fearfully and wonderfully made."* He says of God's Great Book, *"All of our days were fashioned or made for us."* He goes on to say, *"How precious also are Your thoughts to me, O God!"*

As seen in the above scripture, the prophet Jeremiah expands on this thought by relating it to our future and how God desires to work in our lives.

Essentially, God created and designed us to harmonize with His plans and purposes for our lives. God has wired us with our personalities, innate abilities, and spiritual gifts to operate according to His intentions. In one of his epistles, Paul says, *"We have been saved and called with a holy calling, not according to our works, but according to His purpose and grace, which was given to us in Christ Jesus before time began.*[2]

Upon salvation, we enter the Father's predestinated purposes. When we come into a relationship with our Creator, He destines everything to come together so that we can be in sync with whom He created us to be concerning His purposes. In this process, we must continually yield and submit to the work of the Holy Spirit; otherwise, we short-circuit the way He has skillfully wired us. Our lives end up in a mess with nothing going right when we short-circuit His wiring. If we want to discover the life the Creator of the universe has created for us, we must do as Paul wrote, *"We must die daily."* Jesus said something remarkably similar. He said, *"If anyone desires to come after Me, let him deny himself, and take up*

---
[2] 2 Timothy 1:9

his cross, and follow me. For whoever desires to save his life will lose it, but whoever loses his life for my sake will find it."[3]

Getting involved with God's purposes is what keeps us going as He works in us both to will and to do for His good pleasure. When our hearts are fully engaged and consecrated to Him, He works on our behalf to align us with His sovereign purposes. Engaging with God with consecrated hearts enables His sovereignty to meet our free will and prepares us to be entirely coordinated with Him and His sovereign goals. God is so concerned that He continually searches the earth for those whose hearts are fully committed to Him in this manner.

Psalm 14:2 *The Lord looks down from heaven upon the children of men to see if there are any who understand, who seek God.*

2 Chronicles 16:9 *For the eyes of the Lord run to and fro throughout the whole earth, to show Himself strong on behalf of those whose heart is loyal to Him.*

Those who seek God and come in sync with Him are like David, who served the purposes of God for His generation. They are like Paul, who said at the end of his life, *"I have fought the good fight and have finished the race."* Will this be your testimony at the end of your life? Or will you short-circuit the way God wired you? The choice is yours. No one can make it for you. Many lives will end in ruin because they tried to re-wire His wiring. They will have excuses just as those who made excuses to Jesus. But as Jesus said, *"Let the dead bury their dead, but you go and preach the kingdom of God."*

Let the encouraging words of the prophet Jeremiah spur you on to seek God and His purpose for your life with all your heart, as the following verses after the opening passage urge us to do.

Jeremiah 29:12-13 *Then you will call on Me and go and pray to Me and find Me, and I will listen to you.* [13] *And you will seek Me and find Me when you search for Me with all your heart.*

---

[3] Mark 8;35

When convinced that God's thoughts toward us are precious and wonderful, we can wholeheartedly embrace all He has destined us to walk in and abandon ourselves entirely to Him.

Prayer

Heavenly Father, help me as You work Your will in me to do Your good pleasure. Help me know Your thoughts toward me are lovely and filled with goodness. Help me fight the good fight of faith as I go forth, fulfilling what is in store for me. Help me follow hard after You in all things as I focus on You.

Poem: In Sync to Fulfill

Destined to fulfill the Father's call, we stride.
Fearfully, wondrously made, our voices rise.
Acquainted with our ways, He draws near.
Wired by God's design, His purpose clears.

From heaven's heights, He seeks hearts to know.
Saved and summoned, predestined paths we go.
Yielding to the Spirit's fire, vessels blaze.
Vision becoming reality, in sync, we go in grace.

Divine roots going deep, thoughts shape to fulfill.
With the mind of Christ, in His purpose we thrill.
Doubts questioning, we stumble in circuitry undone.
In mercy's hands, rewiring—His masterpiece begun.

Course altered, back on track, we humbly tread.
Accepting precious thoughts, our thoughts spread.
Confident, we press forward, His cross embraced.
In sync with Him, we die—to life fully graced.

Scriptures to Meditate Upon

Psalm 139:13-17, 2 Timothy 1:9, Romans 8:29, Hebrews 12:9, Ezekiel 36:27, 1 Thessalonians 5:19, Philippians 2:13, 1 Corinthians 15:31.

~

May God bless you richly as you ponder what it means to be in sync with all He has destined for your life.

Day 5
Delighting in God's Great Love

John 3:16 *For God so loved the world that He gave His only begotten Son, that whoever believes in Him might be saved.*

Jesus was the perfect expression of the Father's great love. The fact that our Heavenly Father gave us Jesus as a sacrificial Lamb to take away our sins and present us spotless to Him is the most significant expression of love that has ever been given.

Jesus constantly portrayed the Father's love as He went forth in ministry to those considered outcasts who needed to be wrapped in His love. Jesus expressed the warmth of the Father's heart exquisitely when He said, speaking of the children of Israel, *"How often I wanted to gather your children together, as a hen gathers her chicks under her wings."* Our Heavenly Father above wants nothing more than to indulge us in the warmth of His great love as He wraps us under the shadow of His wings. He deeply desires to keep us as the apple of His eye as we hide under the shadow of His wings.[4]

As we faithfully meditate upon His great love, He reminds us of His goodness and wonderful works toward us. In doing so, He satisfies our longing souls and fills our hungry hearts with His goodness. Daily, reminded of His beautiful thoughts towards us just as David was, our faith in Him grows more potent.

Psalm 139:17 *How precious also are Your thoughts to me, O God! How great is the sum of them!*

As we focus on God's beautiful thoughts toward us, He draws us into greater intimacy with Him while we bathe in His tremendous

---

[4] Psalm 17:8

love. By continually setting our hearts on things above rather than earthly discomforts and trials, He lifts us above all that is mundane and burdensome.

***Colossians 3:1-3** If then you were raised with Christ, seek those things which are above, where Christ is, sitting at the right hand of God. ² Set your mind on things above, not on things of earth. ³ For you died; your life is hidden with Christ in God.*

To delight in the Father's love is to set our hearts on Him. We delight in His presence by setting aside time daily to draw near to God. We do it proactively through meditation, reading, studying His word, worship, or intercession.

We cannot afford to allow condemnation, guilt, and the pressures of our daily lives to keep us from soaking in His presence. Even though His love and presence are still there, condemnation and guilt block us from sensing it. Our Heavenly Father desires us to come boldly into His presence and experience the warmth and joy that flows from His heart toward ours. As we faithfully come before Him, we sense His love washing over us with revelation and understanding while His wonderful treasures flow freely from His throne above into our lives.

***Psalm 107:8-9** Oh, that the men would give thanks to the Lord for His goodness, and for the wonderful works to the children of men! 9 For He satisfies the longing soul and fills the hungry soul with goodness.*

Prayer

Heavenly Father, I desire to come into your presence today to indulge in Your great love. Help me to put aside worldly concerns as I set my heart on all You have in store for me from Your magnificent treasure house. Release from me all guilt, shame, and condemnation. Help me know that I can come boldly into Your presence with praise and thanksgiving for Your wonderful works.

Poem: From My Window

From my window, God's wonders are seen in the skies.
Expectations of a new day, sunrise is seen as it rises.
How will this day wrap me in the arms of His love?
Sun rising, eyes are blinded by its brightness above.
Gazing upon its beauty, I'm awakened with His love.

Looking out my window, warmth is felt, so bright.
Squirrels playing joyfully without care or fright.
Playing and flying freely, His love joyfully marvels.
In the beauty of His created ones, God's hand reveals.
More than those who chirp and fly, in us, He delights.

From my window, sadness is seen on some passing by.
Homeless walking by, I wonder where they sleep tonight.
Sun fading, gives way to cold and darkness with bite.
I pray the provider supplies as the sun fades away.
Taking note of sadness seen, in prayer, I convey.

From my window, mothers and children joyfully stroll by.
Rejoicing in their little miracles of birth, they sing lullaby.
Gazing upon their beauty, their hearts fill with wonder.
Aware of God's faithfulness, they fill with gratefulness.
Taking note of God's beauty and wonder, I give praise.

Looking out my window, stray cats bask in the sunlight.
They sleep contentedly, well-fed, though they've no home.
The neighborhood their home; they disappear into the night.
Giving thanks, I give praise for the impact of a stray cat.
In awareness, I realize I'm more significant in God's sight.

Looking out my window, all seen, I fill with amazement.
Seeing His handiwork, I rejoice in all made for enjoyment.
Looking with care over what's conceived, peace liberates.
Faith arising, His love washes with all He's achieved.
Wrapped in His tender love of care, the moment is enjoyed.

Scriptures to Meditate Upon

Matthew 6:24-34, Psalm 17:8, Romans 1:20, Psalm 107:8-9, Colossians 3:1-3, Hebrews 4:14-16.

~

May God bless you richly as you enter His presence, and He showers you with the precious thoughts He has reserved especially for you.

Day 6
Communicating Your Faith

Philemon 1:6 *that the sharing of your faith may become effective by the acknowledgment of every good thing which is in you in Christ Jesus.*

What is it that God has called you to do? It is through the sharing or the communication of our faith that it becomes effective. As we share or confess to others the acknowledgment of every good thing we have in Christ Jesus, we grow and mature in our faith and calling. Therefore, instead of communicating the negatives of life with others, we must change our communication pattern to what we believe to be accurate – all of which we have in Christ.

Ephesians 1:17-20 *That the God of our Lord Jesus Christ, the Father of Glory, may give you the spirit of wisdom and revelation in the knowledge of Him, [18] the eyes of your understanding being enlightened; that you may know the hope of His calling, what are the riches of the glory of His inheritance of the saints, [19] and what is the exceeding greatness of His power toward us, according to the working of His mighty power [20] which He worked in Christ when He raised Him from the dead and seated Him at His right hand in the heavenly places.*

Let me ask you a question. Do you daily experience the exceeding greatness of the power of the Holy Spirit—the same power that raised Christ from the dead? Probably not. I know I'm not. It is His will and desire for all of us. We may experience it in varying degrees at times, but for the most part, we are still lacking. Why is that? Could it be that we do not fully believe to the point we are entirely convinced in the same manner that Abraham was? He was wholly persuaded, without wavering by what God had promised. He believed God would perform on his behalf. Like Abraham, it takes a fully confident heart filled with Bible-believing faith to possess everything pertaining to life and godliness in Christ.

Paul also walked in the faith of Abraham by basing his confession on what he believed rather than any doubts and uncertainties that may have arisen from time to time. His confession was, *"And since we have the same spirit of faith, according to what is written, 'I believed, and therefore I spoke,' we also believe and therefore speak."*

We grow from faith to faith when we base our faith on the covenant promises God has given through His word rather than a list of failed experiences. We must speak and confess according to His word rather than our experiences. God's word says He has given us everything pertaining to life and godliness. We must believe and, therefore, speak as Paul did. Faith is released when we believe and speak according to God's ability and sufficiency rather than our insufficiencies. Believing and speaking accordingly is the kind of faith we must communicate daily. Our belief in what God gave us must be woven into the fiber of our beings. As a result, words of faith will flow freely from our lips as we are faithful in communicating what is in our hearts. The question is, do we believe in the promises of God? Have we set our hearts on them?

Our Heavenly Father is waiting for us to unlock all the treasures He has in store for us through the communication of our faith. Ask Him today, believing in the promises given through His great covenant of salvation. All His promises are yes and amen.

Prayer

Father God, I open my heart to You today as I go forth in all You have purposed for me. Please help me acknowledge every good thing you have placed in my life. Help me To speak according to Your word rather than circumstances that sometimes seem contrary to all You're doing. Therefore, I commit my path to Your ways today.

Poem: Speaking with a New Heart

The slate wiped clean, we speak with a new script.
All made things new, His wind blows upon the spirit.

New reflections on life, we speak accordingly.
No longer caught in meaningless chatter, we speak.
His word filling: we speak new things into existence.

Blood cleansing, we speak according to the hope within.
No longer judged by the past, we confess His greatness.
As conquerors, we believe in the majesty of His power.
In His inheritance, we speak according to His calling.
Acknowledging every good thing, He leads triumphantly.

In the same spirit of faith as Jesus, we believe and speak.
Confession no longer based on uncertainties, we walk.
No longer driven by the past, His word, we communicate.
Fully convinced of His promises, we go from faith to faith.
Knowing He leaves nothing undone, we acknowledge.

Amid uncertainties, His word a lamp, we move forward.
Given all things in life, we speak according to the promise.
As He cares for lilies and birds, we speak accordingly.
No thought for provision, we speak according to His word.
Without worry, we walk by faith, believing, and speaking.

By faith in His covenant promises, we believe and speak.
Wavering not in unbelief, we press towards the promise.
With promises, yea and amen, we rise to the challenge.
Resting in His sufficiency, we trust and speak boldly.
Divine abilities at work, we acknowledge all good things.

Psalm 107:31 *Oh, that men would give thanks to the Lord for His goodness and for His wonderful works to the children of men!*

Scriptures to Meditate Upon

Romans 4:20, 2 Corinthians 4:13, 5:17, 21, Hebrews 9:14, Romans 8:37, 2 Corinthians 2:14, Psalm 119:105, Matthew 6:25-34, 2 Peter 1:2-3.

~

May God bless you richly as you thank Him for all the goodness He provides. May you unlock the treasures He has for you through the communication of your faith.

Day 7
Clearing the Way Forward

Hebrews 12:1 *Therefore we also, since we are surrounded by so great a cloud of witnesses, let us lay aside every weight and the sin which so easily ensnares us, and let us run with endurance the race that is set before us.*

As Christians, most of us are still carrying some clutter from the past. God's will toward us is that we rid ourselves of all the clutter in our lives so that we can freely pursue the destiny and purpose He has charted out for us.

When we come to Jesus, He fills us with joy and anticipation of our new commitment. However, as we press forward in this newfound faith, we realize we have weights holding us back. Our past bondages prevent us from moving forward. Before we can partake and enjoy the fabulous treasures from the Father's great treasure house, we realize how important it is to deal with our past.

Before coming to Christ, our lives were littered with all kinds of clutter that must be removed. Whether sexual impurities, failed marriages, financial blunders, addictions, unforgiveness, broken relationships, divorce, emotional wounds, abandonment issues, various cases of abuse, disappointments, or whatever, we need freedom from all that oppresses. Jesus came to deliver and set free those taken captive by Satan and his devices.

Luke 4:18 *"The Spirit of the LORD is upon Me because He has anointed Me to preach the gospel to the poor. He has sent Me to the brokenhearted, to preach to the captives and recovery of sight to the blind, to set at liberty those who are oppressed."*

To get free from our past, we must believe Jesus desires to heal and set us free; otherwise, our lives will remain cluttered. The Bible says that it is our faith that overcomes the world.[5] Therefore, for the

---
[5] I John 5:4

healing process to begin, we must believe that Jesus desires to heal and make us whole again. Mary Magdalene's story is a beautiful example of Jesus' compassion toward those wounded by the cruelty the world is capable of dishing out. Jesus freed her from the agony of her past and helped her have an extraordinarily successful and rewarding life.

Much of the clutter filling our souls are strongholds God desires to tear down. God gave us spiritual weapons to clear the clutter or the strongholds in our lives to receive the healing and restoration that He desires for all of us. Let us pursue God's recovery plan to be all He has ordained us to be as we give ourselves to His purposes.

2 Corinthians 10:4-5 For the weapons of our warfare are not carnal but mighty in God for pulling down strongholds, casting down arguments and every high thing that exalts itself against the knowledge of God, bringing every thought into captivity to the obedience of Christ.

When strongholds of the past clutter our lives and we do not deal with them, we become agitated in spirit. When agitated, it becomes difficult to focus on the present. For example, whenever I sit down at my desk to work, I first want to clear all the clutter out of the way so I can work from a neat desk. If I do not do this, I become agitated and have difficulty focusing on what I am supposed to do.

All the areas mentioned above produce wounds in us, which Jesus desires to heal. For healing to begin, we must be courageous enough to open and look at the wound. We must understand the destruction wounds cause when we allow them to fester. Once we know the injury, identify and pinpoint where it came from. Then, invite the Holy Spirit, our helper, to deal with it. We then submit to Him in the process as He shows us through His Spirit and the Word what is required. No matter how painful it may be, we must embrace the healing balm the Lord wants to use for our spiritual therapy. The Book of Hebrews gives us some great advice on how to do this.

Hebrews 12:12-13 Therefore strengthen the hands which hang down, and the feeble knees, [13] and make straight paths for your feet, so that what is lame may not be dislocated, but rather be healed.

Making straight paths involves different things depending on your wounding. In many cases, it starts with forgiving the offended party. Then, it means doing what is needed to heal and restore broken relationships. Addictions may involve seeking and confessing the help you need to get free. It also means having a godly sorrow with true repentance.

Whatever your therapy, allow Jesus' compassion and mercy to touch your wound today so that the healing process can begin. Allow the Holy Spirit to burn the clutter and chaff from your lives. He is faithful and incredibly competent in doing so.

Prayer

Father, I come to You today for the help I need in clearing all the clutter that keeps me from experiencing all You have from Your great storehouse. I submit myself to the work of the Holy Spirit as He burns the offending chaff in my life.

Poem: Clearing the Way Forward

Desiring to move forward, stuck in mire, we cry for relief.
Prevented from laying hold, clutter seen, causes grief.
Realization taking hold, the need for removal strikes fear.
Viability blocked: envy, hatred, shame, and lust stand reproved.
Recognized as strongholds, they clutter the way, unmoved.

Immobilized, crying for help, we thirst for liberty.
Denial lifting, we see clutter's damaging negativity.
Taking heed, we acknowledge and confess to others.
Thoughts brought into alignment, hope overflows.
Help given, the Helper supplies what's needed to grow.

Determination absorbing, rising thoughts captivate.
Unbridled thoughts captivating, we arise with dignity.
Mighty weapons given, vision for freedom liberates.

Clearing the Clutter of the Past – Treasurers from Above

Old strongholds disintegrating, liberty releases.
Faith rising with purpose, vision fills with peace.

Fire igniting from kindling's old chaff, vision increases.
Left behind and forgotten; fresh vision intensifies in peace.
Pressing on for the prize, the way forward is unimpeded.
To this end we now strive, His power working in us mightily.
No longer stuck, clutter removed, we move forward readily.

Scriptures to Meditate Upon:

Philippians 2:13, 3:12, 1 Corinthians 6:9-11, Psalm 34:6, James 5:16, 2 Corinthians 2:9-11, 10:4, Ephesians 1:17-19, Matthew 3:11-12, Philippians 3:14, Ephesians 3:20, Colossians 1:29, Philippians 2:13.

~

May God bless you as you allow faith to arise in your heart and go from faith to faith, removing the clutter from your life.

Day 8
Shifting Shadows of Time

James 1:17 *(NIV) Every good and perfect gift is from above, coming down from the Father of the heavenly lights, who does not change like shifting shadows.*

We are living in extraordinary times — whirlwinds of change. Change is happening so fast in today's world it is hard to keep up with all the changes. Some are good, and some are bad. Yet, as the shadows shift with the sun's passage, our Heavenly Father and His eternal values stand unaltered. In a world that's alarmingly transforming, His words remain our steadfast anchor. While today's cultures discard the cherished values of past generations like old newspapers, clinging to the motto, "Out with the old, in with the new," we must be different.

The challenge for every God-fearing Christian is to stay firmly rooted in the righteousness of our Father in heaven amid the chaos of shifting shadows. We live in a season where evil is celebrated as good and good is condemned as evil. Let's not be swept away by the violent tide of wickedness spreading across the globe. We must hold tightly to our faith as the turbulence and disorders of our cultures try to disrupt God's system and calling in our lives.

Jesus warned of the fate of two houses: He said one would be built on sand and the other on rock. Those who build on the ever-changing sands of time will not withstand the torrential storm of evil barreling down on them. But those who are firmly established on the rock of Jesus Christ's Lordship will endure anything that comes their way. As morals and truth crumble, those who build on the Rock will remain unshaken while the world's cultures erode under shifting shadows.

Shifting Shadows of Time – Treasurers from Above

As morals shift, we must resist the world's squeeze by offering ourselves as living sacrifices. We are to focus on the Lord's perfect will, presenting ourselves as living sacrifices. Amid unacceptable practices, we must stay devoted to the Father's will. As false doctrines sweep through our cultures and the Church, we must learn to endure sound doctrine amid all the turmoil. Remember, we have an eternal anchor of hope that keeps us steady in these shifting shadows. Endless treasures of Heaven await all who endure to the end.

Hebrews 10:23 Let us hold fast the confession of our hope without wavering, for He who promised is faithful.

Prayer

Father God, I come to you today asking for strength and stability amid all the changes in our world. Please help me remain faithful and resist the shifting morals of the world. Help me to be salt and light in this dark world.

Poem: Shifting Shadows of Time

With many turbulences and disorders, we navigate.
Shifting shadows deceiving, cultures lie in havoc.
Unbelief, violence, and corruption raging, we're tested.
Holding fast to hope, in shifting shadows, we're tried.
Wavering not, on solid ground, we're protected.

Tried and tested, lives built on the Rock remain secure.
In defiance, lives invested in shadows won't endure.
Investing in shifting shadows, the foolish go astray.
Caught in collective reasoning, they stand in dismay.
Yielding to shifting shadows, they grope in disarray.

Righteousness is considered evil, shifting shadows threaten
In diabolic outpour, they come, brutal despisers of good.
With evil considered good, they fulfill their wanton desires.

Many departing the faith, blasphemers have their way.
Deceiving spirits released everywhere, many fall prey.

Morals declining, deceit and deception strike multitudes.
Hearts growing cold, deception leads to denial by myriads.
Drunk in their desires, they march foolishly to destruction.
Marching to what's seemingly right in their eyes, they stray.
Paths of turmoil striking, holy ones are caught in the fray.

Shifting shadows resisted, sound doctrine discerns.
Watchful, not given to demonized thoughts, we stand firm.
Diligently, rightly dividing truth, we abide in righteousness.
Shunning profanity and vain babbling, we endure to proclaim.
Departing all iniquity, in His righteousness, we stand firm.

With eternal homes prepared for the faithful, He gives hope.
Shadows giving way to a world falling apart, there's an anchor.
With hope as an anchor, peace comes amid shifting shadows.
As the storm rages, hope in the eternal is steadfast and sure.
Holding fast to our confession, He who is faithful delivers.

Scriptures to Meditate Upon

Matthew 7:24-27, Matthew 24:12, Proverbs 14:12, 2 Timothy 3:12-13, John 16:33, 2 Timothy 3:1-5, Isaiah 5:20-21, 2 Timothy 2:15-16, 1 Timothy 4:1, John 14:1-4, Hebrews 6:18-19.

~

May God bless you mightily as you give yourself to the One who holds you in the shadow of His wings during shifting shadows of time.

Day 9

Dining With Jesus

Revelation 3:20 *Behold, I stand at the door and knock. If anyone hears My voice and opens the door, I will come into Him and dine with him, and he with Me.*

One of the more intimate pictures of Jesus and His disciples is that of the Last Supper. As the disciples dine with their Master, His beloved disciple, John, leans upon Him in a distinct expression of intimacy.[6] John is the supreme example of the Father's intimacy with all His children throughout the Gospels. The picture of the Last Supper illustrates this perfectly.

Our Heavenly Father desires that we all come together in the same level of intimacy these early disciples experienced with Jesus. The Scripture above illustrates how we are all invited to sit at His table to dine with Him. Just as John leaned upon Him, He desires us to lean upon Him daily as we receive all He has to offer while sitting and dining in His presence.

I come from a large family. There were eight of us, including our parents. We had regular mealtimes together every day of the week. As we sat around the table, we all had our places at the table. It was our seat at the family table. I can still remember my position at the table. Just as I had my seat at our family table, our Heavenly Father desires to give us our very own seat at His table, where we can enjoy intimacy with Him and the other family members. Here, we discover our place and function in this great family. Just as each member of my natural family had specific chores and responsibilities, so it is with the family of God.

---

[6] John 13;23

Whether you have experienced the intimacy of a natural family or not, it is not necessary to be a part of our Heavenly Father's great family. God sets the solitary in families.

Psalm 68:5-6 *A father of the fatherless, a defender of widows, is God in His holy habitation. ⁶ God sets the solitary in families: He brings out those who were bound into prosperity, but the rebellious dwell in a dry land.*

John 1:12 *But as many as received Him, to them He gave the right to become the children of God, to those who believe in His name.*

We must never forget that God, the Father, seats and arranges us around His table. He is intimately acquainted with all our ways and knows whom we need to be seated with. He knows our gifts and talents and what it takes for them to come to fruition.

1 Corinthians 12:18 *But now God has set the members, each one of them, in the body just as He has pleased.*

From our place or position the Father has placed us in, we minister one to another as good stewards of God's manifold grace. As we faithfully and continually minister from this position, regardless of our season, He continuously supplies and provides for our needs from His treasure house.

Psalm 36:8 *They are abundantly satisfied with the fullness of Your house, and You give them drink from the river of Your pleasures.*

Prayer

Father, as I come into Your presence today, I desire to dine with You and receive all You have for me as I go about my day. Help me keep my mind on You as I drink from the river of Your pleasures. Help me be open to the opportunities that come my way, and help me be a good steward of Your manifold grace.

Poem: Dining at the Father's Table

Unformed, our days were fashioned when nonexistent.
Filled with questions, we search concerning existence.
With exquisite food set, the Father invites to His table.
Coming into His presence, we ponder where to recline.
With answers to His mysteries, He fills us while we dine.

Invitation responded to, we rejoice exceedingly in glee.
Finding our place, nourished, and encouraged, He sets free.
Saved according to His purposes, we freely go in His Name.
Embracing the cross, dying to self, we welcome His will.
Like flames of fire, He empowers, ministering to fulfill.

Gifts discovered, He reveals deeper levels of sensations.
Intimately acquainted with our ways, the Father positions.
In places fashioned in Him, He knows the gifts needed.
Seated accordingly, we're fitted and framed into place.
From our chosen place at the table, He sends in His grace.

As seasons come and go, new gifts and talents revolve.
Creative abilities once locked open as ministries evolve.
Continuing to dine with Him, He abundantly supplies.
No longer concerned about the future, we embrace His love.
Oh, what pleasure continually dining at the Father's table.

Scriptures to Meditate Upon

Psalm 23:5-6, Psalm 139:3,16, Ephesians 1:17-19, Matthew 16:24, 1 Corinthians 12:4-7, Ephesians 4:7, Ephesians 4:16, 1 Peter 4:10, 2 Corinthians 9:8-10, Matthew 6:25-34.

~

May God bless you richly as you go forth from His table, giving out of the abundance that has been freely given to you.

Day 10
Fulfilling God's Purposes

A crucial key to living a victorious Christian life is remaining committed to God's purposes throughout our sojourn here on earth. It takes one who is fully committed to His purposes to keep the oil of His Holy Spirit continually flowing into our lives and to maintain the level of fervency needed to fulfill all commissioned to us through the Holy Spirit.

Whatever our station in life is, God has called us according to His purpose and grace. Whether we are full-time ministers, workers in the marketplace, homemakers, construction workers, migrant workers, police, firefighters, librarians, students, blue-collar workers, or professionals, we are all called to work out His purpose in our lives.

2 Timothy 1:9 Who has saved us and called us with a holy calling, not according to our works, but according to His own purpose and grace, which was given to us by Christ Jesus before time began.

Three of the principles and commands God gave in His word to help us stay fully committed to His divine purposes on earth are as follows:

Believing in the Promises of God

Just as Abraham believed in the promises of God, and it was accounted unto him as righteousness, so must we.[7] To stay committed to God and His purposes throughout our sojourn here on earth, we must believe He will perform on our behalf just as He has promised through His word. As seen on the next page, when we believe God for His promises, it produces His glory working in us as vessels unto honor.

---

[7] Romans 4:20-22

2 Corinthians 1:20 *For all the promises of God in Him are Yes, and in Him Amen, to the glory of God through us.*

When we believe in God's promises and His ability to perform on our behalf, we move forward with passion, enthusiasm, and zeal as we fulfill His word. Through His love, fervency, and anointing, His gives us the ability to engage the enemy, knowing we have total victory over him. We are fearless as we trample over him with all the power and authority Jesus gives us.

Luke 10:19 *Behold, I give you the authority to trample on serpents and scorpions, and over all the power of the enemy, and nothing shall by any means hurt you.*

What are the promises of God you need to believe in so that God can work on your behalf today? Spend some time today meditating on them as you go about your day.

Presenting Ourselves as Living Sacrifices

Presenting ourselves as living sacrifices means our overall lifestyle will be an example of dying to self-daily by taking up the cross of Christ.

Romans 12:1 *I beseech you, therefore, brethren, by the mercies of God, that you present your bodies a living sacrifice, holy acceptable to God, which is your reasonable service.*

What is on your path today that demands sacrifice? Be willing to embrace the cross of Christ, even though it may be uncomfortable. As you do, it will be a step of faith leading you to the next step. As it says in Romans, *"The righteousness of God is revealed from faith to faith; as it is written, 'The just shall live by faith.'"*[8]

Not Entangled with Worldly Affairs

Because we are in this world but not of it, we will be touched by worldly things in one degree or another. If we give into them, they become snares, interfering with our passion and calling. When we become more enthusiastic about worldly pursuits than seeking God

---

[8] Romans 1:17

and His kingdom, we risk committing spiritual adultery.[9] Our worldly desires and entanglements then become idols and snares to us. If we lack passion for God and his kingdom, we should ask ourselves, "What has stolen our passion?"

2 Timothy 2:3-4 *You, therefore, must endure hardship as a good soldier of Jesus Christ. [4] No one engaged in warfare entangles himself with the affairs of this life that he may please him who enlisted him as a soldier.*

As people who are passionate and desire to be a part of all God is doing as He builds His vast army of soldiers for Christ, we cannot afford worldly pleasures and pursuits to taint our pursuit of God and His kingdom's purposes. They are nothing more than spiritual affairs that lead us to spiritual adultery and away from being fully committed to God.

As you ponder how these three principles fit into your daily life, ask the Lord to give you wisdom and strength to obey Him in all things as you go forth as His kingdom ambassadors.

Prayer

Father, I come to You today in humility, confessing that I need You as my helper to believe in Your wonderful promises. Help me embrace Your cross as I present myself as a living sacrifice unto You. Help me to put aside those worldly things and thoughts that pull me away from Your divine purposes so that I may please You in all things.

Poem: Freely Committed to the Cause

Saved according to God's purposes, He draws.
Filled with excitement and wonder, we pause.
With hearts engaged, we come with expectations.
Tasting His goodness, we commit to His operations.
With hungry hearts, we ask for manifestations.

In humility, embracing Christ's attitude, we emulate.
Hearts freely and entirely committed; we speculate.

---

[9] James 4:4

Counting the cost, fully embracing, we sacrifice.
Worldliness renounced, kingdom pursuits, we embrace.
Filled with wonderment; we give ourselves to His cause.

From heaven above, He finds those seeking.
Will we be those whom He finds, we wonder.
Counting the cost, fully committed, He discovers.
Discovering what's ahead, we communicate.
Fully set on His purposes, we occupy to dominate.

No longer bound, we untangle from worldly affairs.
Decisions based on kingdom realities; we rejoice.
No longer my will, but His will, we give generously.
Walking circumspectly, time redeems for His desires.
Freely committed, we bask in His goodness.

Hearts fully engaged; we discover His gifts.
Behaving like Christians, we walk in obedience.
Fervent in spirit, we rejoice in hope.
Patient in tribulation, we count it all joy.
Sensitive to others, we cling to His goodness.

Scriptures to Meditate Upon

1 Peter 2:1-3, Luke 14:27-30, Psalm 14:2, Romans 12:1-2, Romans 12:9-21, 2 Timothy 2:1-4 Mark 14:36, Ephesians 5:15, Matthew 6:19-21, 33.

~

May God bless you as you give yourself to Him wholeheartedly in all that you do.

Day 11
The Goodness of God

Psalm 139:17 *How precious are Your thoughts to me, O God. How great is the sum of them!*

The above Scripture perfectly expresses God's goodness to each of us. The Father fills us with His thoughts toward us, and goodness flows freely from His throne into our lives as we give ourselves wholeheartedly to Him.

One of the greatest joys in life is the birth of a new child coming forth from the womb. When the child is born, the hearts of the new parents fill with gratitude and joy. Their thoughts towards this young child are precious, with goodness and warmth pouring forth from their loving hearts, as expressed by our Father, God.

When we are born again by God's Spirit, our Heavenly Father and all the angels in Heaven rejoice over us. The Father's heart fills with nothing but goodness and warmth toward us. His many thoughts toward us are precious. As the apple of His eye, His thoughts are full of peace and a future as He plans our ways.

Jeremiah 29:11 *For I know the thoughts I think toward you says the Lord, thoughts of peace and not of evil, to give you a future and a hope.*

Our hearts are encouraged as we grow and mature in His great love towards us. We discover the wonders of His grace and how His goodness continually flows from His heart to ours. When God's goodness flows into our lives, we sense the shame of our past dissipating as it sets us free. Through His goodness, He replaces past strongholds with His righteousness, which secures us, even in times of trouble. His goodness acts as a guardrail to keep us safe and protected from all evil.

Nahum 1:7 *The Lord is good, a stronghold in the day of trouble, and He knows those who trust Him.*

As His goodness fills our hungry hearts, we are filled with insight, revelation, and wisdom as we see through the eyes of His Spirit. Through the Holy Spirit, He gives us the ability to discern every good thing and His wonderful thoughts towards us. With spiritual eyes opened, we perceive His calling and gifts as we work out this great salvation in godly fear as He pours freely into us. As His goodness envelops us, He continually leads us in repentance. The more we understand the goodness of God, the more He draws us into the wonderful treasures from above.

Through His goodness, He refreshes our souls daily as we meditate on how great His goodness is. Because He has come into our lives to relieve our weary souls, we place our trust and confidence in Him. He earnestly desires to refresh us daily with His goodness springing forth to all who call upon Him.

As we draw from the wells of His salvation, His goodness pours forth in many ways. He continually satisfies our longing souls and fills our hungry hearts with His goodness. In the process, He heals, delivers, and fills us with hope and encouragement as we go forth into the battles of life. The goodness we experience in this life is a foretaste of all we will encounter throughout eternity.

***1 Corinthians 2:9-10** But as it is written: "Eye has not seen, nor ear heard, nor have entered into the heart of man the things which God has prepared for those who love Him." ¹⁰ But God has revealed them to us through His Spirit. For His Spirit searches all things, yes, the deep things of God.*

God promises to reveal everything He has in store for us through His goodness. The Holy Spirit constantly searches the Father's heart for all He desires to pour into our lives from His awesome treasure house, now and throughout eternity. Ask Him to open your eyes to experience the spirit of revelation and His goodness toward you.

Prayer

Father, I come to You in the name of Your Son, the Lord Jesus Christ. Open my spiritual eyes and fill me with the revelation of everything You are preparing for me now and throughout eternity.

Poem: The Goodness of God

Free to all, the goodness of God springs forth from love.
Those responding, He fills with newness from above.
Bound in guilt, shame, and self-hatred, we overcome by love.
Goodness received, new insight and revelation flow freely.
Hearts wide open, freedom from terrors flow fearlessly.

In a moment, warmth fills as goodness and hope abound.
No longer drowning in sorrow, He places us on solid ground.
Like a mighty rushing river, we're cleansed with forgiveness.
Giving way, streams of living water pour from abundance.
From newness within, turmoil disappears into hearts of peace.

Like a guardrail, the goodness of God comes with security.
Righteousness in place, peace holds firm in disparity.
A stronghold in the day of trouble; anxiety and tension disappear.
Though storms come, waves of peace wash away all agitation.
Hope filling, its anchor holds steady while storms rage on.

Goodness taking root, body, soul, and spirit experience healing.
Where sickness and disease exist, healing enters for all.
Healing taking root, sin, and wounds give way to regeneration.
Where destruction was, now comes redemption from the fall.
Oh, that God's people would give thanks for His goodness to all.

Scriptures to Meditate Upon

Luke 15:10, Ephesians 1:17, Acts 3:19, John 14:27, Hebrews 6:19, Psalm 103:1-5, Psalm 107:1-9, Romans 2:4.

~

May God, the Father's richest blessings, be upon you as you give yourself to the discovery of all that He has destined for your life.

Day 12
The Beauty and Majesty of Knowing God

Psalm 145:3 Great is the Lord, and greatly to be praised, and His greatness is unsearchable.

One of life's greatest pursuits is discovering God in all His glory and majesty. This discovery enables us to come into a deeper understanding and revelation of who God is. It allows us to experience His wonderful attributes coming alive in our hearts, resulting in greater intimacy with Him. We can see with the eyes of our understanding the wonders He has prepared as we partake of all that He has for each of us on this incredible journey.

Psalm 27:4 *One thing I have desired of the Lord that will I seek: that I may dwell in the house of the Lord all the days of my life, to behold the beauty of the Lord, and to inquire in His temple.*

Many of us grew up with misconceptions about who God is. As a result, we may have been afraid of getting too close to Him. We may have had false perceptions of God in how we have viewed authority figures, including our fathers or mothers. We tend to project onto God the unloving characteristics of those who have influenced our lives.

How we perceive God will affect how we relate to Him. Therefore, it is of the utmost importance that we have a correct Biblical view of who God is. It is essential to see and perceive God in the way He has revealed Himself through His word because every aspect of His word is pure and equips us to be complete in Him. A correct Biblical view allows us to see and perceive God as someone who likes and loves us no matter what we have done. The following Scripture reveals the bottom line of how God genuinely thinks about each of us as individuals.

Beauty and Majesty of Knowing God – Treasurers from Above

Jeremiah 29:11 *For I know the thoughts that I think toward you says the LORD, thoughts of peace and not of evil, to give you a future and a hope.*

When we begin to perceive God in the same way He perceives us, there is an agreement in the Spirit that brings us to a deeper level of intimacy and understanding with Him. This new level of intimacy causes us to seek Him with a heart of assurance that desires to come boldly into His presence rather than shrink back in fear and intimidation. The following two verses from Jeremiah reveal this:

Jeremiah 29:12-13 *Then you will call upon Me and go and pray to Me, and I will listen to you. ¹³ And you will seek Me and find Me when you search for Me with all your heart.*

A true revelation of God in His transcendent and personal attributes helps us appreciate and place a higher value on our new relationship with our Father in heaven. It enables us to willingly embrace Christ's mind and attitudes—God's divine nature.

We ultimately become a reflection of who we believe God to be. Many misrepresent God because they lack a proper understanding of who He is. Jesus perfectly represented the Father because He knew Him in all His transcendent and personal attributes. He came to reveal the true heart of the Father. Speaking of Jesus, the following Scripture says:

Hebrews 1:3 *Who being the brightness of His glory and the express image of His person and upholding all things by the word of His power, when He had by Himself purged our sins, sat down at the right hand of the Majesty on high.*

When we look at the beauty and majesty of God's creation, especially when we see some of the world's natural wonders, we can only imagine the beauty and magnificence that await us as we enter the eternal realm. As we open our eyes to all He has created, we cannot help but believe in God, who is so magnificent in everything He does.

A new Heaven and earth await all who trust and believe in the Lord Jesus Christ. As the sun, moon, and stars reveal His glory, we set our hearts on Him in whom dwells all the fullness of the Godhead bodily.

Beauty and Majesty of Knowing God – Treasurers from Above

Romans 1:20 *For since the creation of the world His invisible attributes are clearly seen, being understood by the things that are made, even His eternal power and Godhead, so that they are without excuse.*

Because God's greatness is beyond discovery. He wants us to discover His creative beauty in our lives, which helps to point us toward our destiny and keeps us on track as we journey along the path that holds the keys to our future. May the Lord's beauty and fascination be with us as we journey toward our destiny in Him.

Ask the Father to reveal His heart to you as you search the Scriptures to discover His greatness and divine nature. As we discover who God is, we come to know Him as He has revealed Himself to us.

Prayer

Father, I pray that you would fill me with your wisdom and knowledge of who You are as I seek to know You in your majesty and glory. Help me to know You as You have revealed Yourself in Scripture.

Poem: The Treasures of Knowing God

Intimately acquainted with all our ways, He's forevermore.
Knowing thoughts, dreams, fears, sins, and more, He restores.
Wherever we go, nothing is hidden, yet His love remains.
Towards us, His thoughts are more than can be numbered.
Brought into captivity, our thoughts remain unencumbered.

May we know Him as He's known us, even in our sin.
With His greatness beyond discovery, we seek to begin.
In His word and creation, hidden keys reveal His majesty.
Hidden treasures discovered; we search with persistence.
Intimacy revealed, we seek without resistance.

In seeking and discovery, misconceptions disappear.
Teaching us, His Holy Spirit reveals His nature, so near.
Pondering beauty and majesty, He reveals His ascriptions.
In His Word, we search out His divine distinctions.
In Word and Spirit, we go forth to uncover all He is.

Beauty and Majesty of Knowing God – Treasurers from Above

In wonder of His creation, His handiwork is discovered.
In beauty and magnificence, His creative zeal is uncovered.
In discovery, He's seen and known in all He's created.
Myriads of stars, streams, mountains, and waterfalls reveal.
In beauty and majesty, He's detected by all who kneel.

In omniscience, He knows futuristically the paths we take.
Going before as a guiding light, He knows what's at stake.
Trusting in God, we navigate through dangers and setbacks.
With thoughts of peace, our future fills with faith and hope.
With more discovered, excellence reveals for His sake.

Incomprehensible and inexhaustible in power, He succeeds.
In omnipotence, nothing too difficult, in power we exceed.
God performing the hard things, our part is attainable.
Not minimizing His power, all things are obtainable.
Discovering and knowing, we're linked to divine ability.

In all that's created, His eternal Godhead, He portrays.
Without excuse, we stand as the sun, moon, and stars display.
Living and moving in Him, intimacy is experienced.
Sun, moon, and stars portraying, we reflect His grandeur.
Knowing He's everywhere, we discover His splendor.

Scriptures to Meditate Upon

Proverbs 2:4-5, 2 Peter 2:2-3, Psalm 139:1-3, 7-8, 40:5, 2 Corinthians 10:5, Proverbs 25:2, Psalm 119:2, John 14:26, Psalm 19:1, Romans 1:20.

Day 13
Spiritual Authority

Hebrews 12:9 Furthermore, we have had human fathers, who corrected us, and we paid them respect. Shall we not much more readily be in subjection to the Father of spirits and live?

Many of us have or have had authority issues. We do not like it when told what to do. I came out of the '60s generation that was very belligerent towards authority. While serving in the Army in Vietnam during the late 60s and early 70s, I was very combative towards authority. It ended with me getting a general discharge for not adapting to military life. My life turned downward for the next few years as I shunned all authority. Thankfully, God, in His mercy, sought me out and brought me to my senses.

I now appreciate and submit to the authorities in my life, especially from the source on high. As Jesus Followers, we are encouraged to submit to the Father of spirits and live according to God's word. It is in Him that we live and move.

Throughout time, God has spoken—sometimes in extraordinary ways and with signs and wonders to get our attention. He spoke through His prophets and His Son, Jesus Christ, throughout Biblical history. All this was to establish His authority on earth as in heaven.

God desires to establish His authority in our lives so we will have the authority and power to carry out His purposes as we minister in His Spirit. For this to happen, we must first be under His rule. To be under His jurisdiction involves humbling ourselves before Him with a contrite heart. It also consists of submitting to those over us in the Lord and submitting to one another in fear of the Lord.

Hebrews 13:17 Obey those who rule over you and be submissive, for they watch for your souls, as those who must give account. Let them do so with joy and not with grief, for that would be unprofitable for you.

Spiritual Authority – Treasurers from Above

In today's Christianity, it seems like many are, once again, under the same spell of Satan that existed during the era of the Judges—a time in which everyone did what seemed right in their own eyes. As a result, the Israelites often fell prey to the enemy's devices and found themselves back under slavery.

Many Christians today are still clinging or falling back to the bondage that comes from the enemy's devices. They are not walking in the spiritual authority God has intended for them. They are not allowing the Word, which is sharper than any two-edged sword, to pierce their hearts with a conviction that enables them to respond obediently.[10] Instead, they are letting the cultural norms of today's world be their guiding influence, just as the Israelites did during the era of the Judges. However, we are urged strongly in the book of Romans not to allow the world to squeeze us into its mold.

Romans 12:1-2 *(Phillips) Don't let the world around you squeeze you into its own mold, but let God re-mold your minds from within, so that you may prove in practice that the plan of God for you is good, meets all his demands and moves towards the goal of true maturity.*

One of the greatest treasures we can receive from Heaven above is our Father's authority, which He earnestly desires us to walk in. Jesus said we have the authority to trample over all the power of Satan when we embrace the authority from on high whole heartedly.

Luke 10:19 *"Behold, I give you authority to trample on serpents and scorpions and over all the power of the enemy, and nothing shall by any means hurt you.*

Before walking in the authority that tramples the enemy, we must bring our fleshly appetites under His control. By allowing our thoughts, actions, and every high thing that exalts itself against the knowledge of God to be brought into the captivity of His word, God must establish His authority in our lives through obedience. When we obey in this manner, we can punish all disobedience and execute spiritual authority as the following Scripture implies.

2 Corinthians 10:4-6 *For the weapons of our warfare are not carnal but mighty in God for pulling down strongholds,* [5] *casting down arguments*

---

[10] Hebrews 4:12

and every high thing that exalts itself against the knowledge of God, bringing every thought into captivity to the obedience in Christ. ⁶ *and being ready to punish all disobedience* ***when your obedience is fulfilled.***

Prayer

Lord, I desire to walk in the spiritual authority You have made available unto me. I allow You to work this out in my life. Help me diligently cast down those arguments that war against my soul. Help me fully submit to You and those You have put in my life to shepherd my soul. Help me be obedient in all things as I trample over all the power and authority of the enemy.

Poem: The Lord Speaks from on High

With flashes of lightning, the Lord speaks from on high.
With all authority, He thunders with power and might.
Standing in awe, we tremble at the sound of His voice.
Held in fear and awe, we ascribe to His glory, so bright.
Drawing nigh, we give ear, eager for passion to ignite.

Spurring us, He calls to come near with contrite hearts.
From blood slain, He invites to approach with boldness.
Welcomed with open arms, He invites to dine in intimacy.
Covered in His robe, we stand in His presence, set apart.
Newness washing over, we gain footing with a new heart.

Obedience to His Word, He shows the way, expanding.
Thoughts higher than ours, we gain new understanding.
Minds renewed; He transforms thorough application.
Given peaceable thoughts, hope comes with expectation.
Approaching boldly, we ask for anything with conviction.

Like flashes of lightning, we convey revelation and insight.
Cleansed and renewed, divine nature is our birthright.
His Word sharp as a two-edged sword; thoughts discern.
With authority given, He takes away unbelief and doubt.
In quietness, His gentle voice instructs for a new route.

Giving praise, we cling to Him, in authority and acclaim.
Recorded in His book, He baptizes us in His great name.

Giving thanks, counted worthy, we bear His Name.
His name recorded, He daily loads with blessings, happily.
As whole-hearted disciples, we become part of His family.

Advancing in faith, we courageously face the unknown.
Filled with purposeful vision, we go, embracing His throne.
With peace and joy filling, we embrace grace, now shown.
Hearts filled, we ascribe Him praise, glorifying His name.
Authority extended in liberty; we embrace works shown.

Scriptures to Meditate Upon

Psalm 29:4, Jeremiah 32:7, Ephesians 1:19-20, Psalm 34:18, Hebrews 4:14-16, Revelation 3:20, 1 Kings 19:12, James 3:17, Jeremiah 29:11-12, Matthew 7:7, Ephesians 1:17, Hebrews 4:12, 1 Peter 1:4, 1 Corinthians 2:16, Psalm 107:8-10, Matthew 28:19, Philippians 4:3, Revelation 17:8, Exodus 20:24b, Psalm 68:19, John 1:12, Luke 10:19-20, 2 Timothy 1:9, John 14:27, Psalm 29:1-2.

~

May God bless you mightily as you go forth in the authority of His Spirit, embracing all that He has for you

Day 14

Embracing the Transformation Process

2 Corinthians 3:17-18 Now the Lord is the Spirit; and where the Spirit of the Lord is, there is liberty. ^{18} But we all, with unveiled face, beholding in a mirror the glory of the Lord, are being transformed into the same image from glory to glory, just as by the Spirit of the Lord.

The Bible calls the transformation process sanctification. Because the term "Sanctification" has brought some confusion to the body of Christ, I choose to use the word "Transformation." The word "Sanctification" simply entails how one is set apart for the Father to use as He pleases. It involves His changing us from glory to glory until the fullness of Christ's stature comes forth in one's life.

One of the essential keys to our growth and maturity in the Lord happens when we understand the transformation process and how it works. As the Holy Spirit transforms us into the likeness of Jesus from glory to glory, He trains our ears to discern His voice while guiding and directing us to be all God calls us to be in Christ. As we yield to the Holy Spirit in this process, He conforms us to the image of Christ, which is a significant part of the Father's predestinated purposes for our lives.

Keeping our eyes on the Lord is the key to staying in this process. As we behold His image in our thoughts, He gradually changes us into His image from glory to glory. By meditating on all His wonderful attributes, the mind of Christ begins to take shape in us as old ways of thinking dissipate, which are a significant key in the transformation process.

Colossians 3:1-2 If then you were raised with Christ, **seek those things which are above,** *where Christ is seated at the right hand of God. ^{2}* **Set your mind on things above,** *not on things on the earth.*

Embracing the Transformation Process – Treasurers from Above

As we set our minds on things above and give ourselves to studying His Word, His ways and thoughts become embedded into our hearts and spirits, transforming and renewing our minds with new perspectives. All things become new as the old gives way to the newness that is now changing us. Our minds fill with new revelation and understanding, with our spiritual eyes open to His wonders. While meditating on the changes the Father desires, the Holy Spirit not only convicts us but helps us formulate plans of action that will keep us accountable to how He intends to bring about the transformation.

When John the Baptist preached his message of repentance, people began looking to him as the coming Messiah. However, as seen in the following Scripture passage, his response helps us understand the root of the transformation process. The fire of the Holy Spirit burns the chaff in our lives.

***Matthew 3:11-12** I indeed baptize you with water unto repentance, but He who is coming after me is mightier than I, whose sandals I am not worthy to carry. He will baptize you with the Holy Spirit and fire. ¹² His winnowing fan is in His hand, and He will thoroughly clean out the threshing floor and gather His wheat into the barn, but **He will burn up the chaff** with unquenchable fire.*

When the Father baptizes us in the Holy Spirit, the fire of God comes to refine us, burning the sinful chaff and changing us from glory to glory. The fire or passion from the Holy Spirit's baptism helps free us from the bondage of addictions. The prophet Isaiah mentions this in a portion of Scripture when He speaks of the **spirit of burning** that causes the Branch of the Lord to be beautiful and glorious.

***Isaiah 4:3-4** And it shall come to pass that he who is left in Zion and remains in Jerusalem will be called holy—everyone who is recorded among the living in Jerusalem. ⁴ When the Lord has washed the filth of the daughters of Zion from her midst, by the spirit of judgment and by the spirit of burning.*

One of the most significant areas of uncleanness we all deal with is the lust of the flesh. These areas continually war against who we are in Christ. As we purpose to walk in the Spirit, we will not succumb to them, with the fire of God constantly burning the chaff of ungodly desires from us.

Galatians 5:16-18 *I say then:* ***Walk in the Spirit, and you shall not fulfill the lust of the flesh.*** *[17] the flesh lusts against the Spirit, and the Spirit against the flesh; and these are contrary to one another so that you do not do the things you wish. [18] But if you are led by the Spirit, you are not under the law.*

Our part in the transformation process is to yield to the Holy Spirit, the One who convicts us of sin. As we respond to His gentle promptings in these areas, He gives us the victory needed, causing us to triumph over lusts that war against the soul. By putting on the characteristics of the new man, the old nature disappears. We find our desires are toward what God is doing in us rather than what is dictated by the lusts of the flesh and the world's cultural norms.

By embracing the transformation process and allowing God's breath to touch our lives, He teaches us to discern His gentle voice and promptings. With this, we experience new liberty in the spirit, causing us to lay hold and cling to the new life that is now setting our hearts on fire. Thus, the Lord's sanctifying process takes root in our lives by being shaped by the Holy Spirit and the word of God.

As the early disciples allowed Jesus to breathe upon them, so must we. However, we must never forget that we have an enemy who wants nothing more than to steal and destroy what has begun to take root in our hearts.

As Paul wrote to the Galatians, *"Who has bewitched you? Are you so foolish? Having begun in the Spirit, are you now being made perfect by the flesh?"* The enemy of our faith will do whatever he can to shift our attention away from relying on the Holy Spirit to rely on our strength and legalistic measures.

When we try to perfect ourselves by any means other than allowing the Holy Spirit to do His work, we produce dead works. We cannot afford to get caught up in dead works created by legalistic measures. They will make us useless in Christ. Our goal is to become Christ's workmanship by allowing the Holy Spirit to produce the actual results. His rewards will last throughout eternity. These are the pure works born from a relationship with the Holy Spirit and God's Word that help those who desire to become vessels unto honor by not allowing the oil in their lamps to diminish.

Ephesians 2:8-10 For by grace you have been saved through faith, and that not of yourselves; it is the gift of God, [9] not of works, lest anyone should boast [10] For we are His workmanship, created in Christ Jesus for good works, which God prepared beforehand that we should walk in them.

Ask the Holy Spirit to breathe on you today as you go forth in the Lord's transformation process. He delights in being your Helper by showing you the way and transforming your life from glory to glory.

Prayer

Father, I invite you to breathe upon Me as the Holy Spirit burns the chaff in my life. Help me conform to the image of Your Son as He transforms my life into Your image.

1 Thessalonians 5:23-24 Now May the God of peace Himself sanctify you completely, and may your whole spirit, soul, and body be preserved blameless at the coming of our Lord Jesus Christ. [24] He who calls you is faithful, who will also do it.

Poem: Transformed Into His Likeness

One offering perfected forever, we're sealed.
Predestined to be conformed to His likeness, we yield.
The work of Christ finished, in His Spirit, we labor.
Giving ear to His voice, He directs and revives.
Fully embracing God's prophetic purposes, we thrive.

Vessels of honor, we seek to be as He purifies.
With unquenchable fire, the chaff burns away.
Walking in the Spirit, fleshly lusts disappear.
Keeping our eyes on Him, He renews and forms.
From glory to glory, in His image, He transforms.

Having begun in the Spirit, the enemy subverts.
Shifting our attention to legalism, Satan beguiles.
Resting in the Word, God protects from his wiles.

Embracing the Transformation Process – Treasurers from Above

With works birthed, we embrace His workmanship.
From glory to glory, He prepares us to be equipped.

With spiritual eyes opened, His wonders never cease.
Submitting to His word, His thoughts are embedded.
With minds filled with insight, newness exceeds.
Submitting to God's authority, the enemy leaves.
Yielding, new nature appears as the old disappears.

Hearts fully engaged; we stretch forth in preparation.
Forgetting the past, we press forward in anticipation.
From glory to glory, the prize within sight, we tread.
As vessels of honor, we engage in prophetic objectives.
Living by His rule, we fully embrace new perspectives.

Embracing invisible treasures, He secures in His love.
Immersed in His purposes, treasures transform from above.
With compelling vision, we discover destiny, now ours.
Transformed into His likeness, we fulfill to give glory.
Filled in His fullness, multitudes inherit all treasures.

Scriptures to Meditate Upon
Romans 8:29, Isaiah 26:3, Psalm 1:1-3, Hebrews 10:14, John 24:26, 20:22, Acts 1:8, Ephesians 2:8-10, Philippians 3:12-14.

~

May the Lord's blessing be with you as you embrace the sanctifying process of the Lord wholeheartedly.

Day 15

Embracing the Peace of God

John 14:27 *"Peace I leave with you, My peace I give unto you; not as the world gives do, I give unto you. Let not your heart be troubled, neither let it be afraid."*

One of our greatest treasures in life is to be at peace with God. When we are at peace with God, we are at peace with the circumstances and events surrounding us. God's peace is eternal, not temporal, like the world's peace, as Jesus adequately reminds us in the passage above.

John mentions two things in the above Scripture that can steal our peace—troubles and fears. First, let us keep in mind that our enemy is a thief. He comes to steal, kill, and destroy. He wants to steal, kill, and destroy our peace with God. He knows if he can do this, he will throw us off balance and cause us to be ineffective in taking the kingdom by force.

Satan uses our troubles to stir up fear rather than relying on our sufficiency in Christ to overcome all situations. The more we rely on our sufficiency, the more we give in to Satan's tactics. On the other hand, when we rely on the adequacy that is in Christ, we activate the abundance of peace and life Jesus has promised us, regardless of our situations and problems.

John 16:33 *"These things I have spoken to you, that in Me you may have peace. In the world, you will have tribulation: but be of good cheer, I have overcome the world."*

When we rest in God and His sufficiency, we release Him to eliminate our fear. His perfect love for us eradicates all fear.

Satan also uses condemnation and guilt to steal our peace. Let's face it; we are all sinners saved by grace. In Christ, He thoroughly cleanses us by His blood and makes us perfect as we stand in His righteousness, which removes all condemnation and guilt from us.

Hebrews 10:14 *For by one offering He has perfected forever those who are being sanctified.*

The above Scripture can release you from all condemnation and guilt once you receive the revelation and understanding of what it entails. Paul makes it clear in his letter to the Romans. He says, *"There is no condemnation to those who are in Christ and walk in the Spirit."* Once freed from condemnation and guilt, God's peace flows like a river, with the enemy of our faith held in check.

The uncertainty of the future and God's ability to provide for our needs can also potentially steal our peace. The enemy works in these areas to trip us up through worry. We must keep our eyes on the promises of God's word rather than the circumstances of our lives if we want God's peace to rule in us.

Jesus encouraged us not to worry by giving no thought to the necessities of life. He said, *"Seek first the kingdom of God and His righteousness, and all these things will be added unto you."* He has given us all things that pertain to life and godliness. As far as our future is concerned, our Heavenly Father wants to provide us with one that is filled with hope.[11] He will be faithful to complete what He has begun in you if you continue to serve Him by seeking God's kingdom first. As a result, His peace will lead you through all things, even the challenging times.

Philippians 4:6-7 *Be anxious for nothing, but in everything by prayer and supplication, with thanksgiving let your requests be made known to God;* [7] *and the peace of God, which surpasses all understanding, will guard your hearts and minds through Christ Jesus.*

Prayer

Father God, I come before You today, asking You to help me keep my mind on You. Help me walk in your peace no matter what circumstances I may face.

---

[11] Jeremiah 29:11

Poem: Embracing the Peace of God

From the wayward way and sin lost within, we moan.
From the heaviness that overwhelms, we stand alone.
Guilt and condemnation engulfing, we agonize in pain.
In helplessness, groping about, we search for peace.
From the torment within, we pray for release.

Behold, the Lamb of God comes, taking sin and shame.
His blood shed, we are cleansed, no longer in flame.
Peace flowing like a river washes torment away forever.
Breathing new life, atonement extends to whomever.
Giving way to peace, sin, and shame disappear forever.

Problems and troubles, like mighty tides, can pull under.
Crying from blunders, taken by His hand, He delivers.
"Oh, you of little faith, why did you doubt and not believe?"
With just a touch, He relieves, reaching out in mercy.
Flooding our souls with peace, He rescues in wonder.

Flooded with uncertainty, the future blurred, anxiety rises.
Looking for security, temptation gives way to compromises.
Clinging to His Word, trust makes way for kingdom surprises.
Leaning on Him, peace that surpasses understanding comes.
Putting God first, His we give place to blessings in sums.

Giving praise to God, we're thankful for the perfect sacrifice.
As our faithful High Priest, He sympathizes with weaknesses.
Giving thanks, we praise Him, who provides for all our needs.
In moments of unbelief, He readily forgives, putting us at ease.
Giving thanks, we praise Him, who fills us with His peace.

Scriptures to Meditate Upon

2 Corinthians 7:6, John 1:29, John 10:10, Romans 8:1-2, 21, 2 Peter 1:3, Matthew 6:25-33, Jeremiah 29:11, Philippians 1:6, 1 John 4:28.

~

May the peace of God rule your hearts as you give yourselves to Him and His kingdom purposes.

Day 16

Breakthrough to the Invisible

John 3:3 Jesus answered and said to him, "Most assuredly, I say to you, unless one is born again, he cannot see the kingdom of God."

God created the world in the beauty and wonder of what was intended to give us glimpses into His eternal treasures. Because of Adam and Eve's sin in the garden, Satan stole this beautiful glimpse of Heaven that was given in the garden. However, God still wants to give us a foretaste of all He created for those who believe in Jesus Christ. The beauty and wonder of these heavenly treasures are sealed in this invisible realm, awaiting to be broken through.

As each of us was born a natural birth that brought us into this world, God desires a spiritual birth to bring us into the unseen beauty and wonder of the eternal realm—the kingdom of Heaven, so that we receive a foretaste of all that was lost in the fall. He's given us a second Adam in Jesus to open our eyes to this invisible realm.

Once we are born again, the Holy Spirit comes to live in us revealing to our natural senses the great mystery of the eternal Godhead in all the God's glory. With His divine nature given, the keys to break through are given to begin our journey into this invisible realm.

Luke 17:20-21 Now, when He was asked by the Pharisees when the kingdom of God would come, He answered them and said, "The kingdom of God does not come with observation; ²¹ nor will they say, 'See here!' or 'See there! For indeed, the kingdom of God is within you."

As Christians, our calling is that of a pilgrimage or journey. The Father desires us to be like Abraham, the father of our faith, who traveled through this world by faith, not knowing where he was going. He was a pilgrim looking for a city unknown to his natural senses—a city whose builder and maker was God, which could only seen through his spiritual eyes. To be like Abraham, we must focus on those things above, wherein all of His wonderful treasures lie.

Breakthrough Into the Invisible – Treasurers from Above

2 Corinthians 4:18 *while we do not look at the things which are seen, but at the things which are not seen. For the things which are seen are temporary, but the things which are not seen are eternal.*

The Christian life is a journey into this invisible realm that has the potential of either being the most exciting and adventurous journey or the most tedious and miserable experience one can imagine. Unfortunately, many default to the latter—not because they wanted to or desired to. It was because they lacked the faith and vision to enter a path invisible to their natural eyes. Jesus said, *"Narrow is the gate, and difficult is the way that leads to life, and few find it."* When we default to the latter, we fail to unlock the treasures and the beauty and wonder that awaits us. As a result, we do not gain a compelling experience of what authentic Christianity entails.

Ask yourself, "Which path has my journey taken me on?"

Your conclusion may be that you have been pushing the default button rather than walking in true faith. If so, do not lose heart because God is with you and delights in revealing authentic faith! He is ready and willing to give you the keys that unlock His treasures. The keys to the kingdom are yours when you step out in faith as Abraham did.

2 Corinthians 5:7 *For we walk by faith, not by sight.*

Ignoring what the natural man sees and hears is a constant battle because it comes naturally to us. We are human beings made up of carnal desires and dreams. It requires faith to see beyond the natural into the kingdom realm, which has the potential to lead us to a life filled with adventure and the abundant life Jesus promised—a life filled with righteousness, joy, and peace in the Holy Spirit.

God initially destined Adam and Eve to live as eternal beings and not experience death. When we are born again, the Holy Spirit, who is infinite, comes to live within us. Death then loses its sting because God has put eternity in the hearts of humanity.[12] It is this eternal realm where God intends for us to live. The problem is we have an enemy who will do whatever it takes to keep us from experiencing

---

[12] Ecclesiastes 3:11

all God intended for us. He knows that once we break past the barrier of unbelief, there is no stopping us from fulfilling the purpose He created for us. We become a threat to Eatan and his domain.

If we are to break past the barrier of unbelief, we must discipline our spiritual eyes to see all God has prepared for those committed to His purposes. But first, we must allow His Spirit access to our inner man. There is exceeding greatness available to those who believe in His mighty power. As we give access to the Holy Spirit, He reveals to our senses the glorious inheritance He desires to provide us with.[13] This power is currently working in us, the same power that caused Jesus to rise from the dead and ascend into heaven.

***1 Corinthians 2:9-10** But as it is written: "Eye has not seen, nor ear heard, nor have entered into the heart of man the things which God has prepared for those who love Him." ¹⁰ But God has revealed them to us through His Spirit. For the Spirit searches all things, yes, the deep things of God.*

We must be courageous and ask ourselves honestly, "Are our steps ordered by the heavenly realm or our natural understanding?" As we allow the Lord to order our steps, our preferences are set on the heavenly rather than the natural, temporal realms.

We must resist the devil and his influences as we submit to God if we are to be kingdom-minded people who reign on this invisible path. Because God yearns jealously towards us, He gives us the ability to journey when we humble ourselves to Him.

Prayer

Father, as I come to You, open my spiritual eyes to Your Invisible kingdom. Guide me into what is prepared for me on this path.

Poem: Breaking Through

Tripping and stumbling, we fall into stagnation.
Seeking more, we seek a Kingdom without observation.
Darkness covering, spiritual eyes unlock invisible spheres.

---

[13] Ephesians 1:16-19

To this realm, free from evil, we flee for what's pure.
Free from darkness smothering, we dwell safe and secure.

Brimming with confidence, we live in the invisible.
With armor given, protective shields appear for security.
Trampling over Satan, new freedom occurs with authority.
In the His secret place, we cling mightily to the Most-High.
With armor protecting, paths revealed, we press to occupy.

Taking the Son's hand, He teaches, filling with assurance.
The Holy Spirit given; He reveals the Father's providence.
Eyes of understanding awakened, we awake in benevolence.
A lamp to our paths, His word gives necessary proficiency.
Trusting in Him alone, we no longer lean on our sufficiency.

Breaking through natural realms, we reign in the unseen.
Spiritual eyes tested, faith evidences invisible realities seen.
In testing and darkness, we cling to His Word in obedience.
Treasuring His Word more than food, we press in persistence.
Holding fast, we press forward, even through disappearance.

With mountains removed, nothing stopping, we press on.
With intrigue and delight, we press hard in anticipation.
Faith to faith, we go; knowing more is seen upon arrival.
Though faith tested, we know we will come forth as gold.
Immersed His faithfulness, He never forsakes in all told.

Living in the invisible, He secures us in His love.
Plans and purposes birthed; perspectives birth from above.
Vision breaking through, we cruise to destiny, now ours. Looking for heaven's city, we discover the builder above.
Knowing upon arrival, He's more majestic than envisioned.

Scriptures to Meditate Upon

Psalms 139:1-3, 7-8, 40:5, 2 Corinthians 10:5, Psalm 145:3, Proverbs 25:2, 2:4-5, Psalm 119:2, John 14:26, Psalm 127:4, 19:1.

~

May God bless you mightily as you press forward in vision and passion for all that awaits you, as go from faith to faith

Day 17

The Wonders of His Grace

2 Corinthians 9:8 *And God is able to make **all** grace abound toward you, that you, **always** having **all** sufficiency in all things, may have an abundance for **every** good work.*

For those of us who have tasted the incredible outpouring of God's love, it's a breathtaking experience. It is an astounding thing to experience the pit He dug us out of and then to know and experience the wonders of His grace that now fill our hungry hearts. We have much to be thankful for all that His grace has accomplished in our lives. We have a Father who is rich in mercy and delights in showing us the wonders of His grace.

Ephesians 2:4-7 *But God who is rich in mercy, because of His great love which He has loved us, [5] even when we were dead in trespasses, made us alive together with Christ (by grace you have been saved), [6] and raised up together, and made us sit together in the heavenly places in Christ Jesus, kl[7] that in the ages to come He might show the exceeding riches of His grace in His kindness toward us in Christ Jesus.*

What we are now experiencing is just a foretaste of the exceeding riches of His grace we will participate in in the ages to come. We have so much to look forward to as He prepares an eternal home for all of us who have come to believe in His Son, Jesus Christ, who poured Himself out as an offering for our sins.

As we allow the Holy Spirit's gentle breeze to blow upon us, He opens the eyes of our understanding to new revelation and insight. We then catch glimpses of what He has prepared for us in this life and the ages to come. Then, finally, His Spirit begins to lift us into the heavenly realms where we are seated with Him—a place where we experience the new life we now see from His perspective. The wonders of His grace fill our minds and hearts as we go forth in the mystery and wonder of His will working in our lives.

The Wonders of His Grace – Treasurers from Above

Because of His great love and grace, the Holy Spirit imparts the mind of Christ, His divine nature, into our spirits. With this, a newfound excitement causes us to quickly put off the old nature bound in sin and shame. Our old clothing no longer fits as we embrace the new. We now clothe ourselves in this new nature as we discard old as filthy rags. With our new clothing in place, we discover His grace is multi-faceted. It's like looking at a diamond with each angle sparkling with discoveries. There is much to learn as the wonders of His grace lead us into His great treasures from above.

With new divine abilities discovered, we go forth with hearts of faith to fulfill destiny and purpose. As we go from faith to faith, more of His treasures are uncovered, motivating us to press forward into all the Father continually pours into our lives. We discover that His grace continuously abounds towards us, with His sufficiency or divine abilities in all things, giving us an abundance for every good work.

As we trust in the reality of God's word and the promise seen in the opening passage, faith erupts in our hearts, exploding with the wonders of His grace working mightily in us as we reach forward to the things ahead. Even though we may not have attained all God has for us, we keep reaching forward in faith, knowing His word is accurate. Paul's testimony of reaching forward is found in the following passage of Scripture.

Philippians 3:12-14 *Not that I have already attained, or am already perfected: but I press on, that I may lay hold of that which Christ Jesus has also laid hold of me.* [13] *Brethren, I do not count myself to have apprehended; but one thing I do, forgetting those things which are behind and reaching forward to those things which are ahead,* [14] *I press toward the goal for the prize of the upward call of God in Christ Jesus.*

May this be the testimony of our lives as we reach forward in the wonders of His grace. May our hearts be filled with faith as we experience the Father's great treasures from Heaven above.

Prayer

Heavenly Father, I thank You for the extraordinary grace You poured into my life. Help me to discover every facet of your grace as I move toward the goal of the upward prize that awaits me at Your coming. Pour Your divine abilities so that I am filled with Your sufficiency in all things rather than my sufficiency.

Poem: The Wonders of His Grace

Caught in an avalanche of sin and shame, we cry out.
Unable to focus, we wander in darkness, full of doubt.
Is there a way out of misery faced through tears?
Unable to cope with lost hope, we cry for deliverance.
In the bleakest of moments, rays of light appear.

A bright morning star, the way revealed, is discovered.
Gentle breezes blowing the wonders of grace, we yield.
As sin and shame disappear, His fragrance unseals.
With profound effects, the weary soul lightens and heals.
God's Son taking reign, reveals wonders of grace.

Condemnation and guilt released; we rejoice in relief.
No longer smothered, anxiety gives way to belief.
Unmerited favor saving, weariness shrivels from avalanche.
His wonders of grace touching, peace floods unmeasured.
Sensing newness in purpose, levity appears, unfettered.

Mind renewing, newness emerges with new identity
Revelation surging, hearts fill in vision and destiny.
Divine nature imparted, senses enlighten and refine
Eyes opened wide, spiritual treasures fill the mind.
Gratitude given; His wonders fill in abundance.

Steps taken into His wonders of grace; faith resolves.
No longer blinded by works of the enemy, fear dissolves
Freed from sin, divine abilities appear from faith.
Grace abounding in good works, our hearts rejoice.
Seed supplied, wonders of grace multiply abundantly.

From desperation to jubilation, our hearts rejoice
Brought so far from the avalanche, we give voice.
No longer beaten down by sin and shame, grace exceeds.

The Wonders of His Grace – Treasurers from Above

Led in triumph over life's issues, grace succeeds.
Touched by His His grace, all glory to God, exceeds.

Scriptures to Meditate Upon

Psalm 34:6, Job 38:7, Romans 8:1-2, Philippians 4:6-7, Romans 6:6-8, 2 Peter 1:2-4, Ephesians 1:17-19, 1 John 4:18, 2 Corinthians 9:8-10.

~

May God bless you with the exceeding riches of His grace as you stay true to His word. He is faithful and will do it.

Day 18

Making the Most of Life

James 4:13-15 Come now, you who say, "Today or tomorrow we will go to such and such a city, spend a year there, buy and sell, and make a profit"; ¹⁴ whereas you do not know what will happen tomorrow. For what is your life? Even a vapor appears for a little time and then vanishes away. ¹⁵ Instead, you ought to say, "If the Lord wills, we shall live and do this or that."

One of the greatest treasures we have from above is the life God has given to us. Do you treat your life as a treasure God gave, or do you take it for granted by not making it count? Are you happy and content with your life, or are you looking for something more than what you have? Are you making the most of the life God gave you, or are you simply spinning your wheels in frustration and discontentment?

We have little time to make our lives count for something. Most of our time spent should be on doing something worthwhile rather than spending our precious energy on things of little value or consequences. Most of us have an inborn need and desire to be valid. We all search for the meaning of existence and need to know there is a purpose in what we do. We need to feel that the tasks and responsibilities we perform are essential. We want them to count. The average person is probably discontent with how their life is going, even though God has promised a rewarding life filled with excitement and purpose.

Psalms 16:11 You will show me the path of life; in Your presence is fullness of joy; At Your right hand are pleasures forevermore.

One of the essential elements of having a meaningful life is staying connected to God's purposes, to which God called us. When we connect to His purposes, we fully discover our unique vision and purpose, which gives us our reason for existence.

Making the Most of Life – Treasurers from Above

***2 Timothy 1:9** who has saved us and called us with a holy calling, not according to our works, but according to His own purpose and grace which was given to us in Christ Jesus before time began.*

A life without purpose causes many to chase endless rainbows, bringing dissatisfaction, heartache, and disillusionment. This results in a sense of failure, apathy, emptiness, and worthlessness. When Solomon lost sight of God's purpose, the things in his life became worthless and futile. As a result, he became dissatisfied and discontent with his life, as seen in the passage below.

***Ecclesiastes 2:10-11** Whatever my eyes desired, I did not keep from them. I did not withhold my heart from any pleasure, for my heart rejoiced in all my labor, and this was my reward from all my labor. ¹¹ Then I looked on all the works that my hands had done and on the labor in which I had toiled; and indeed, all was vanity and grasping for the wind. There was no profit under the sun.*

We must look to God's purpose in all that we do. We need to see what we do as God-given tasks, understanding that God wants to work His purpose in all things. By acknowledging Him in all our ways, He will continually direct our paths in the fullness of His joy. As we acknowledge Him in all things, it keeps us from chasing empty rainbows. If my dream is an end, it becomes a pointless pursuit.

We must ask ourselves: "Why am I disappointed and dissatisfied? What is going on, that is making me feel this way? Why am I not making the most of my life? Are my priorities out of order? Am I putting more time and energy into areas that have little consequences? Should I put more time into my family, marriage, and service to God?"

__Proverbs 21:5 The__ plans of the diligent lead surely to plenty, but those of everyone who is hasty, surely to poverty.

As we commit all our ways to the Lord, He establishes our thoughts. Our courses are then planned according to His purposes for our lives. As a result, we make the most of our lives while we count for something other than meaningless existence. You were born for a purpose far beyond meaningless existence, so embrace who you are in Christ and dedicate yourself to His purposes. You will not only have a meaningful life but one filled with joy and peace. You will have a life that counts dearly to all you encounter.

Prayer

Heavenly Father, I come to You today, asking for Your help in committing my ways unto You. Help to me keep Your purposes always before me as I do my daily tasks.

Poem: As Years Go By

As the years go by, we count blessings one by one.
Looking back, we stand in awe of all God has done.
Lives in His hands, He brings forth what's concealed.
Many run in circles, chasing rainbows, while others yield.
Those bearing fruit yield to the eternal weight of glory.

As years go by, many stand in wonder, nothing achieved.
Regret in life wasted, nothing is counted for or conceived.
Sadness fills with wonderment, of what could've emerged.
If only the voice within was heard rather than submerged.
Living for today, so enticing; nothing gained or enlarged.

As years go by, we understand our lives are but vapor.
Here today, gone tomorrow, little time making life matter.
The eternal weight of glory, we yield for life, so pure.
God's will or ours, ultimate decisions to discover destiny.
No regret, those yielded store treasures throughout eternity.

Help us, Lord, taking eyes off self, turning to You in all we do.
Help us in seeing Your eternal weight of glory, making us anew.
Help us to make our lives count for something so holy and pure.
Help us come to the end of ourselves in all we endure.
Help us be forever grateful for all that You do in and through.

Scriptures to Meditate Upon

Proverbs 29:18, Ecclesiastes 3:19-13, Proverbs 3:6, 16:3, 9.

~

May God bless your day mightily as you give yourself to His ways.

Day 19

The Kingdom Powered Life

Luke 17:20-21 *Now, when He was asked by the Pharisees when the kingdom of God would come, He answered them and said, "The kingdom of God does not come with observation; ²¹ nor will they say, 'See here, or see there!' For indeed, the kingdom of God is within you."*

Jesus came to reveal a kingdom not coming by observation, meaning it would be an invisible yet am authentic domain in which to live and reign. To take full advantage of all that His kingdom offers, submission to the Lordship of Jesus Christ and His governing authority is a necessity, which is based on the principles and commands given to us throughout the word of God.

1 John 3:22 *And whatever we ask, we receive from Him because we keep His commandments and do those things that are pleasing in His sight.*

Our Heavenly Father's great desire is to lavishly pour out His kingdom blessings, giving us everything that pertains to life and godliness. It is through these blessings that He transforms us into Christ's image, working in and through us.

When we are born again, the Holy Spirit enters our lives to begin this transformation process that delivers us from the powers of darkness to convey us into His kingdom blessings. First, however, we must submit to the process; otherwise, we quench His Spirit and stifle the transformation process.

When controlled by carnal, earthly desires from the kingdom of darkness, we frustrate the grace of God. As a result, we are not fully translated into the realm of His Son. We get caught in the tug-of-war for control of our souls. If this is so, we cannot expect to enjoy the kingdom's blessings and benefits the Father desires to daily load upon us. Therefore, the Book of Hebrews says, *"Shall we not much more readily be in subjection to the Father of spirits and live."* We are strongly urged in Scripture not to allow the world to have a hold on us by squeezing us into its mold. Who is winning the tug-of-war with your life? It is whoever you are yielding to the most.

1 John 2:15-16 *Do not love the world or the things in the world. If anyone loves the world, the love of the Father is not in Him* [16] *For all that is in the world—the lust of the flesh, the lust of the eyes, and the pride of life—is not from the Father but is of the world.*

Satan will do everything in his power to keep a hold on us. As we submit ourselves to God's authority, Satan releases his grip on us as James, the Lord's brother, encourages us in His letter. He says, *"Therefore submit to God. Resist the devil, and he will flee from you."* As we humble ourselves in the sight of God, He lifts us to a kingdom perspective that transforms our lives. The Lord orders our steps as we set our affections on His kingdom realm. The question is, are our affections set on the heavenly realm or the natural, temporal realm? Kingdom-minded people resist the devil and his influences.

The Father wants to open our eyes to the fullness of the spiritual treasures He desires to pour into our lives. As we receive from His heavenly storehouse, He fills us with an abundance of all that belongs to Him. With the eyes of our understanding opened, we receive a deposit of faith to go forth as fully equipped ambassadors of His kingdom.

When we embrace the kingdom-powered life, we experience the divine abilities that transform us from glory to glory. New levels of freedom come from each paradigm shift as we change from glory to glory. Not only do we receive the motivation to change, but we also gain the power to change. We realize we are no longer enslaved to sin but renewed by the kingdom's power within.

As kingdom principles shape our hearts and minds, we discover life decisions are made from kingdom perspectives rather than earthly ones. In the process we learn to lean on God's ways rather than our limited understanding. We discover His understanding, and perspectives are much higher and better than ours. Therefore, we depend upon Him in all things.

Prayer

Father, today, I submit myself to Your governing authority as I go forth as an ambassador of Your kingdom. Work Your will and desires in me as I give myself to all You want to accomplish in and through me. Release me from any holds the enemy still has on me that I may be more than a conqueror in all things.

Poem – Kingdom Living

In this world but not of it, we live and reign.
With thoughts shaped by His Word, we press to gain.
Minds stayed on Him; directing our ways, we trust.
With spiritual eyes opened, His treasures disperse.

In obedience to Word and Spirit, we live and move.
Faith in Word and promises, we lay hold to prove
In obedience, our hearts reap and enjoy abundance.
Committed to His ways, thoughts establish in substance.

Called according to His purposes, we walk with tenacity.
Embracing God's purposes, He fills with vision and destiny.
With our heart's desire realized, we serve enthusiastically.
With blessings, we stand in awe; faith renewed ecstatically.

In difficulty, we persevere and trust His faithfulness.
Holding fast, we treasure His Word in all told.
Deeper perception released, we come forth as gold.
With joy and resolve, we press forward to behold.

Governed by stewardship, we give faithfully.
Sowing into His Kingdom, we reap now and eternally.
Casting our bread upon the water, we reap as it unfolds.
Daily loaded with benefits, His authority takes hold.

Abasing or abounding, we give thanks in all measures.
He who supplies makes rich according to His treasures.
As faithful ambassadors of His Kingdom, we give praise.
Causing us to triumph, we give glory in all adventures.

Scriptures to Meditate Upon

Hebrews 12:9, Matthew 7:21, Colossians 1:12-13, 2 Peter 1:2-4, 1 Thessalonians 5:19, Psalm 68:19, Romans 12:1-2, James 4:7, Colossians 3:1-2, Matthew 6:33. 2 Corinthians 3:18.

~

May the Lord lead you daily with benefits! As you go forth with an abundance for every good work, may you be fully equipped in Him.

Day 20

Avoiding the Snares of the Enemy

Psalm 140:5 *The proud have hidden a snare for me, and cords; they spread a net by the wayside; they have set traps for me.*

In Christ, we are given much. We have many treasures to lay hold of, now and throughout eternity. As a result of hearing the joyful sound from His Spirit, we have been given love, joy, peace, and righteousness in the Holy Spirit. We serve our Father God, who delights in daily loading us with the benefits or treasurers from His kingdom. He has given us everything we need that pertains to life and godliness. As Jesus said, *"I have come to give you a life filled with abundance."* In the same breath, He also said we have an enemy who wants nothing more than to steal, kill, and destroy what we have through God's great love and grace.

We must take the threat of our enemy seriously. Peter says in one of his epistles, *"Be sober, be vigilant: because your adversary the devil walks about as a roaring lion, seeking whom he may devour."* Many easily fall prey to the enemy's devices simply because they have not clothed themselves in the Lord's garments. They are still walking according to worldly customs rather than obeying God's word. They have not put on the protective clothing that comes from submitting to the Lordship of Jesus Christ. The weak are easy pickings for Satan with the traps he sets for those who think they are strong in their misguided ways.

King David understood what was in the heart of the wicked and how they worked. Therefore, he took great precautions to be vigilant against their tactics. His confession is as follows:

Avoiding the Snares of the Enemy – Treasurers from Above

Psalm 119:110-112 *"The wicked have laid a snare for me, yet I have not strayed from Your word. [111] Your testimonies I have taken as a heritage forever, for they are the rejoicing of my heart forever. [112] I have inclined my heart to perform Your statutes forever, to the very end."*

David knew how to avoid the snares of his enemies. He allowed God's testimony about who He was to be His stronghold. As a result, David resolved in his heart to hold fast to the Lord to the very end. He made an unwavering commitment to avoid the unsuspecting snares the enemy put in his path. We must do the same to avoid the enemy's traps. When we put our trust and confidence in the Lord through obedience, He guides us away from the enemy's snares.

Even though David had a strong testimony, he was not perfect and fell into Satan's traps on more than one occasion, just as we do. Fortunately, the Lord was able to release him from the snares. Because he quickly repented, he was released when confronted with His sin. The key to getting released swiftly from a snare after falling prey is to promptly repent and come boldly to the throne of grace to obtain mercy and find the help needed in a time of need. A righteous man gets up immediately, clothed in the righteousness of Jesus.[14]

Paul tells us in his first epistle to the Corinthian church that temptations are common with all of us. He says that God will provide a way of escape from temptation. The question is, do you know your way to escape amid your temptations? Satan may set his traps, but God has given us a way around them. He's given us His word as a lamp unto our paths. David said, *"Your word I have hidden in my heart that I may not sin against You."* When Satan tempted Jesus, He quoted the applicable Scriptures that applied to His temptations.

I think most of us know the temptations we deal with continuously. The question is, do we have specific Scriptures that deal with the temptations in our hearts? We will not become entrapped by the enemy's snares if we do. Instead, we will walk right around them

---

[14] Proverbs 24:16, Hebrews 4:14-16

as we call the Scriptures hidden in our hearts into remembrance. Hiding Scriptures in our hearts is part of what it means to gird up the loins of our minds and be sober, as Peter encouraged us in His first epistle.

One of our most excellent defenses against Satan and his snares is to go on the offensive by diligently adding the fruit of the Spirit to our faith. In Peter's second epistle, he lists character traits similar to what Paul gave to the Galatians that we need to add to our faith. Peter then sums it up by saying, *"Therefore, brethren, be even more diligent to make your call and election sure, for if you do these things, you will never stumble."*

Prayer

Father, I come to You today for help. Help me not to be ignorant of the enemy's devices. Awaken my senses to know the traps he sets for me. Help me see the escape routes that take me away from temptations attempting to overpower me. Be with me as I purpose to make my calling and election sure.

Poem: The Snares of the Enemy

Hearing the joyful sound from His Spirit, we delight.
In light of His countenance, we walk in His might.
Lifted above the circumstances of life, we rejoice.
No longer controlled by concerns, we lift voices.
Hearts set accordingly, we treasure His abundance.

All given by God, the enemy comes to steal.
Setting traps, he seduces as thoughts swirl.
Subverting what's true, distractions conceal.
Sabotaging, he drags into pits of depression.
Falling into self-pity, he snares into transgression.

Struggling for deliverance, none seem to care.
Turning their backs, we sink deeper into despair.
Submerged in snares set secretly, we cry for rescue.
Setting hearts on Him alone, He releases from snares.
Released, hearts set, we praise Him for His care.

Avoiding the Snares of the Enemy – Treasurers from Above

Words fitly spoken; He rescues with encouraging words.
Though Satan sets traps, we trust God and His precepts.
Watching our paths, He knows ways to be kept.
Testimonies of those before us, we set as our heritage.
Countenances lifted; we rejoice in truths mastered.

Hearts inclined to His word, forever we proclaim.
To the end, we follow Him, who rescues from regret.
To Him who sets free, we give thanksgiving and praise.
Blessings flowing, He guides around traps set.
In joyfulness of His Spirit, our countenance resets.

Scriptures to Meditate Upon

Psalm 89:15, John 10:10, Psalm 142:3-7, Romans 13:14, 1 Peter 5:8, Proverbs 24:16, 1 Corinthians 10:13, Psalm 119:11, 105, Matthew 4:1-11, 1 Peter 1:13, 2 Corinthians 2:10-11.

~

May God bless you mightily as He leads you around the snares the enemy secretly sets in your way.

Day 21

Abiding in His Presence

Revelation 3:20 *Behold, I stand at the door and knock. If anyone hears My voice and opens the door, I will come in and dine with him, and he with Me.*

Victorious living during our Christian pilgrimage here on earth is an innate desire we all possess. Abiding in the presence of the Holy Spirit is the primary key to flourishing in the Lord's presence. He desires to commune with us daily, which involves a desire on our part as much as it does from Him. We must respond to His invitation. He is always there, no matter what the situation we may be facing. As the Scripture says, *"He will never leave nor forsake us."*[15]

Even though we don't always sense His presence, we must carry on as if we do. We walk by faith and not by sight or feelings. John gives good insight into what it means to abide in His presence.

John 15:4-5,7 *"Abide In Me, and I in you. As the branch cannot bear fruit of itself unless it abides in the one, neither can you, unless you abide in Me, ⁵ I am the vine, you are the branches. He who abides in Me, and I in him, bears much fruit; for without Me, you can do nothing. ⁷ If you abide in Me, and My word abides in you, you will ask what you desire, and it shall be done for you."*

The above passage shows how we are to abide. Jesus said that to abide in Him is to allow His words and commandments to abide in us. Allowing His commands to direct our lives, we cleave to Him as the word *"abide"* implies. King David's expressed this well. He said, *"Consider how I love Your precepts; revive me, O Lord, according to Your loving kindness. I rise before the dawning of the morning and cry for help; I hope in Your Word. My eyes awake*

---

[15] Hebrews 13:5

through the night watches, that I may meditate on Your Word."[16]

We have so much in today's world that distracts us from keeping our minds focused on the Lord. Our world is inundated with sensory overload. The entire world lies in the lap of our enemy. He uses every device and tactic known to humankind to keep us from abiding in the presence of the Lord. Because he knows where our strength and joy come from, he will do whatever he can to keep us distracted.

What are the things that distract you from setting your heart on the Lord's abiding presence? Are you taking the time each day to allow His word to revive your heart and mind? When you do, it gives you a jumpstart into your day with your thoughts set on the Lord. The more we purpose to keep our thoughts on the Lord, the more we sense His abiding presence. Managing our thoughts implies bringing them into the captivity of His word as we meditate on all that is true and good, as Paul encouraged the Philippians to do.

Philippians 4:8 *Finally brethren, whatever things are true, whatever things are novel, whatever things are just, whatever things are pure, whatever things are lovely, whatever things are of good report, if there is any virtue and if there is anything praiseworthy—meditate on these things.*

Most of what we see and hear through the media and airwaves are the opposite of what Paul expressed in the above Scripture. It is a challenge to sense the Lord's abiding presence when our minds get constantly bombarded with the lies, filth, and violence that fill the airwaves. Yet, that is what we tune into daily rather than girding up the loins of our minds to be sober and vigilant. We then wonder why we do not have peace of mind. If we want His abiding presence, we must be proactive by setting our hearts and minds accordingly. It would be helpful to list the specific things that relate to your life that Paul spoke of in the above Scripture so that you immediately have them at hand when your thoughts begin to stray.

When we abide in His presence, the unexpected things that happen to us do not catch us off guard. Instead, they allow us to respond as Jesus would, knowing He is always there, no matter what. Abiding in His presence enables us to discover His treasures pouring into our

---

[16] Psalm 119:159

lives as He gives us sufficiency in all things.

Prayer

Father, I ask You today to help me keep my thoughts focused on You rather than the meaningless chatter of the world.

Poem – You're Always There

Like a dragnet, we're often caught in webs of false illusions.
You're there to stop us in our tracks despite our delusions.
Crying out in mental anguish, You're there to dismantle.
In Your patience and loving-kindness, we remain joyful.
Teaching to trust, we know You're always there to untangle.

Thoughts turning, You're there in the quiet of the night.
Trusting, faith, and confidence fill our hearts with might.
In guidance and faithfulness, You assist through the day.
In dependability, You're there when thoughts stray.
Observing closely, You're there, even in our failures.

As the enemy comes to destroy what's given, you succor.
Amid the turmoil, You're there when anxiety coerces.
Though Satan plunders, You provide from earthen treasures.
Surprised, we stand in awe and wonder at how You produce.
In Your faithfulness, we continually trust in Your measures.

Giving thanks, we look to You, who keeps your eyes focused.
You're always there, watching with such tenderness.
Blessed beyond measure, You pour forth in benevolence.
Forever grateful, we stand in Your mercy and indulgence.
Never leaving nor forsaking, we trust, knowing You're there.

Scriptures to Meditate Upon

Psalm 34:6, Psalm 9:10, Proverbs 3:5-6, Deuteronomy 7:9, Matthew 6:26, John 10:10, 2 Corinthians 4:7, Matthew 6:33, Matthew 23:37, Psalm 91:4. Hebrews 13:5.

~

May God bless in keeping your thoughts focused on whatever is lovely and pure.

Day 22

Discovering Your Destiny and Purpose

2 Timothy 1:9 *who saved us and called us with a holy calling, not according to our own works, but according to His own purpose and grace, which was given to us in Christ Jesus before time began.*

When you think about your purpose and destiny, what comes to mind? Do you believe you were born with a future and purpose to fulfill, or were you destined for meaningless existence? The truth is God created us to play a particular role uniquely designed according to our personality, gifting, innate abilities, and talents we possess, as well as the many experiences, whether good or bad, we picked up along the way. Only as we willingly enter the role God has designed for us can we fully engage in discovering all He has created us to be and do. When we willingly embrace this role, we experience the abundant life He has promised to us.

It is essential to understand everything God creates is with a purpose. When He created you, He had a definite goal related to His purposes on the earth, as seen in the following Scripture.

Jeremiah 1:5 *"Before I formed you in the womb, I knew you; before you were born, I sanctified you; I ordained you a prophet to the nations."*

We may not be called to be prophets to the nations, but just as God knew Jeremiah before He formed him in the womb, He also knew you and me. He had a role already ordained for Jeremiah, just as He does for all of us, who are called according to His purposes.

The question is, are we living the role God designed for us, or are we lost and wandering souls still looking and searching for what life is all about and coming up empty?

Discovering Your Destiny and Purpose – Treasures from Above

Proverbs 20:5 *The purposes of a person's heart are deep waters, but one who has insight draws them out.*

Our purposes and destinies are locked away in our hearts. As we seek God and His purposes with all our hearts, the Holy Spirit begins to draw them out. He is incredibly good at unlocking the hidden areas of the heart that hold the keys to all He has purposed for our lives. When this discovery becomes our life ambition, we release what is in the deep waters of our souls.

1 Corinthians 2:9-11 *But as it is written: "Eye has not seen, nor ear heard, nor have entered into the heart of man the things which God has prepared for those who love Him." [10] But God has revealed them to us through His Spirit. For the Spirit searches all things, yes, the deep things of God. [11] For what man knows the things of a man except for the spirit of the man which is in him? Even so, no one knows the things of God except the Spirit of God.*

To properly connect with our destiny and purpose, we must understand that God is always at work, bringing us to where we can discover and capture the destiny He has marked for us.

Henry Blackaby, the author of "Experiencing God," says, *"When God gets ready for you to take a new step or direction in His activity, it will always be in sequence with what he has already been doing."*

It is important to understand that we all have defining or kairos moments when God allows us to see things from His perspective. By viewing our lives through this lens, we get glimpses of our calling and destiny. We see this illustrated in the life of David.

When looking at the life of King David, it is easy to see how the defining or kairos moments of his life were all leading him in the same direction as he discovered his purpose and calling. The account of David's great battle with the giant, Goliath, illustrates what it means to take a forcible charge of your destiny when you glimpse God's perspective and purpose at a defining moment. It is also important to note that David had many defining moments leading up to one of his greatest kairos moments.

David had a good reason for responding with a heart of faith at his critical moment when he met Goliath. He had already looked to his past and recognized the kairos moments leading up to this great conquest. So, when he went before King Saul to convince him he was up to the task, he began recounting his past experiences. He as able to access his past to give him a greater understanding of what God was doing in the present. They were clear signposts that ushered him into this moment.

1 Samuel 17:36 *Your servant has killed both lion and bear; and this uncircumcised Philistine will be like one of them, seeing he has defied the armies of the living God.*

One of his earliest defining moments that led to this was when the prophet Samuel appointed him the next king. I wonder how often God had already spoken to his heart alone with his flock of sheep, playing his harp and singing before the Lord? Samuel's word to him was more than likely already in his heart when he spoke to him concerning becoming the next king.

Following David's conquest with Goliath, a series of defining moments brought David into a deeper walk with God and added broader dimensions to his faith. It was from faith to faith that David entered his destiny. As we set our hearts to claim our future, it is the same for us.

Romans 1:17 *For in it the righteousness of God is revealed from faith to faith; as it is written, "The just shall live by faith."*

Review your life from your earliest memories and think about how they have shaped you into the person you are today. What are the innate abilities and spiritual gifts that have shaped you? What is your personality type? All of this is God's handiwork in your life. What are some of the experiences, good or bad, that have shaped your life? Do you see a common thread that God has woven through all of this? Give this some thought as you go about your day. May God bless you as you capture what has been hidden away in the recesses of your heart.

Prayer

Heavenly Father, I open my heart to You today to fulfill Your purpose. Please remind me of all that You do in my life.

Discovering Your Destiny and Purpose – Treasures from Above

Poem: Destiny in Mind

Lost in mazes of unbelief and pity, we cry for relief.
Through fogs of unbelief, we often lose the way.
Where to turn when gripped in blindness?
Lost without hope, we grope in darkness.
Looking for rays of light showing the way, we pray.

In the distance, small rays appear on the horizon.
Trying to access hidden areas of the heart, we ponder.
To open wider for to shine through, we consider.
To unlock areas closed before we collapse, we muse.
Disillusion ruling, before time elapses, we ponder.

Curiosity winning, we dare to peek at what's exposed.
Light bursting through, vision appears unopposed.
Revelation filling our minds, new light sheds.
Peace and joy flooding, vision for tomorrow renews.
Hearts filling with promise, we commit to paths ahead.

Committing to Christ above, vision and purpose converge.
No longer blinded; in faith, we reach for what's ahead.
Failures and disappointments forgotten, forward we tread.
From faith to faith, the way forward is continually revealed.
Confidence filling: vision, purpose, and destiny converge.

Scriptures to Meditate Upon

Psalm 139:1-3,16-17, Philippians 1:6, Romans 8:28, Jeremiah 29:11, 2 Timothy 1:9, Proverbs 29:18, John 16:13-24, Philippians 3:12-14.

~

May God bless and enrich your life today as you give yourself to all He has destined for you to walk in. May you lay hold of that which Christ has already laid hold of for you.

Day 23

Sowing Seeds of Faith

Ecclesiastes 11:6 *In the morning sow your seed, and in the evening do not withhold your hand; for you do not know which will prosper, either this or that, or whether both will be good.*

No matter what season we are in, we must continue to sow seeds of faith with the expectation that God will honor our efforts. Walking through the dark tunnels of life, we wonder, "Will we ever see the light at the end of the tunnel?" Job was in such a predicament when he cried out to the Lord and said, *"Look, I go forward, but He is not there, and backward, but I cannot perceive Him; when He works on the left hand, I cannot behold Him; when He turns to the right hand, I cannot see Him. But He knows the way that I take; When He has tested me, I shall come forth as gold."*

Job was a man of faith who continually sowed seeds of faith regardless of his circumstances. The secret to his faith was that he kept putting one foot before the other. Even though he could not see the light at the end of the tunnel, he continually held fast to the steps of the Lord, even in his darkest moments. By treasuring God's word more than his necessary food, he found the light at the end of the tunnel. His testimony was as follows.

Job 23:10-12 *But He knows the way I take; when He has tested me, I shall come forth as gold. ^{11} My foot has held fast to His steps; I have kept His way and not turned aside. ^{12} I have not departed from the commandment of His lips; I have treasured the words of His mouth more than my necessary food.*

As a result of sowing seeds of faith in his darkest moments, God rewarded Job abundantly. God restored his losses by twice as much as he had before the great trial of his faith. He received a double portion.

Job's faith erupted despite the dark tunnel he went through because he had already spent time sowing seeds of faith by getting to know God's heart towards Him. As a result, he could keep his eyes on the big picture rather than the momentary affliction he was experiencing. As the apostle Paul wrote to the Corinthians, the eternal weight of glory produces faith in our hearts.

2 Corinthians 4:17-18 For our light affliction, which is but for a moment, is working for us a far more exceeding and eternal weight of glory, [18] while we do not look at the things which are seen, but at the things which are not seen. For the things which are seen are temporary, but the things which are not seen are eternal.

Job's testimony was, *"Though He slays me, yet will I trust Him."* Whatever season you are in, now is the time to sow seeds of faith. You never know when you may need an eruption of faith. He who sows little reaps little. He who sows much reaps much. As we learn to trust God in the little things, we sow seeds of faith for the more significant issues in life. The words from the prophet Jeremiah reveal the importance of sowing seeds of faith in the simple things of life.

Jeremiah 12:5 if you have run with the footmen, and they have wearied you, then how can you contend with horses? And if in the land of peace, in which you trusted, they wearied you, then how will you do in the floodplain of the Jordan?

Because faith comes by hearing, and hearing comes through reading and studying God's word as He breathes on it, we must give ourselves to it. If we want the kind of faith Paul spoke of and Job had, we must believe the entirety of God's word is inspired by Him and profitable for equipping our faith. As a result, our faith will erupt when needed, just as Job's did.

When we continually sow seeds of faith in every aspect of our lives, we will always have what is needed for our present circumstances. Whether in times of abasing or abounding, we will be content, knowing God is at work producing in us an eternal weight of glory. From His eternal treasure house, He pours what we need for the moment into our lives. Our part is to trust in His provision and to be content.

Prayer

Father God, help me walk in the faith of a Job as I go forth into all You have for my life. Help me recognize when I need to be sowing seeds of faith to have what I need during difficult times.

Poem: Faith Erupts

Coming to You at times, there's fogs of unbelief.
Without condemnation, You always give relief.
Trusting in You, faith refreshes our spirits, unstopped.
Reminded of Your greatness, thoughts stay focused.
Your love nourishing our troubled souls, faith erupts.

Amid life's trials pulling down, unbelief corrupts.
Looking downward, we're blinded to what's promised.
As mountains in the distance, Your promises stand true.
Eyes refocused, we're free from molehills of unbelief.
Lifting eyes to all that's promised, faith erupts.

Situations contrary to Your word, unbelief settles.
With confusion and delusion, false perceptions battle.
In agreement with Your Word, peace within levels.
Humbly admitting falsification, we trust Your word.
With faith and trust in Word's purity, faith erupts.

Amid the soul's dark moments, Your image decreases.
Unbelief tempting, darkness gripping, visibility ceases.
Holding to Your word, stepping forward, we lay hold.
With light shining ahead, we come forth as gold.
Treasuring Your word as necessary food, faith erupts.

Without vision, casting off restraint, unbelief corrupts.
With renewed vision and purpose, eyes open wide.
Sensing and engaging Your Spirit, we walk side by side.
Faith leading to unknown conquests, we cease losing heart.
Communicating Your works of righteousness, faith erupts.

Scriptures to Meditate Upon

Proverbs 3:5-6, Hebrews 11:6, 2 Corinthians 9:6, Job 13:15, Colossians 3:1, 2 Peter 1:2-4, 2 Timothy 3:16-17, Job 42:10.

Sowing Seeds of Faith – Treasures from Above

~

May God increase your faith mightily in all you do as you go forth in the strength of His Spirit. May your faith erupt during those timely moments in your life when it is needed the most.

Day 24

The Renewing of Our Minds

Romans 12:2 *And do not be conformed to this world, but be transformed by the renewing of your mind, that you may prove what is that good and acceptable and perfect will of God.*

From the Father's great treasure chest, He gave us everything pertaining to life and godliness. To fully take advantage of all that God has given us through our relationship with His Son, Jesus Christ, requires that our minds be renewed. Before coming to Christ, our minds, attitudes, and characters were shaped according to worldly thinking. God has now translated us from the kingdom of darkness into the kingdom of the Son. This transformation process changes how we think about everything. As seen in the above reference, Paul speaks of this transformation process in his epistle to the Romans.

God's thoughts and ways are vastly different and foreign to how most of us were brought up to think. We operated out of a carnal mindset until we accepted Christ as our Lord and Savior. God's ways are much higher than our carnal ways of thinking. Therefore, our minds needed renewing according to His thoughts based on eternal perspectives.

Isaiah 55:9 *For as the heavens are higher than the earth, so are My ways higher than your ways, and My thoughts than your thoughts.*

If we are to succeed as His kingdom ambassadors, it is expedient that we become spiritually minded. The Father desires to impart His divine nature or the mind of Christ so that we will know how to think and navigate in this new Heavenly kingdom dimension. Unless our minds are transformed and renewed, the way we think remains warped. We are then caught in a tug-of-war between Satan's domain and the kingdom of God. Until full conversion takes place by having our minds renewed, we cannot break free from Satan's grip.

The Renewing of Our Minds – Treasures from Above

The Father has given to His Holy Spirit and the word of God—the Bible to help us in this transformation process. With His Spirit and His word working together, we are unstoppable. The Holy Spirit, our helper, searches the heart of the Father to reveal His ways to our new thinking processes. With His word as a lamp unto our paths, we can move forward into the uncharted territory of His kingdom domain. As we commit our thoughts to Him, He establishes our ways of thinking.

The primary attitude needed to continually move forward in this transformation process of having our minds renewed is humbling ourselves as little children.

*Matthew 18:2-4 Then Jesus called a little child to Him, set him in the midst of them, ³ and said, "Assuredly, I say to you, unless you are converted and become as little children, you will by no means enter the kingdom of Heaven. ⁴ **Therefore, whoever humbles himself** as this little child is the greatest in the kingdom of heaven."*

Many have problems when coming to Christ, because they are unwilling to discard their old ways of thinking. When I fully surrendered my life to Christ, I had a lot of strange ideas about God and who He was. However, I realized those ways of thinking had not gotten me anywhere nor produced the quality of life I desired. Therefore, I consciously decided to humble myself and put my former thoughts on a shelf. I did not want what I was learning about Jesus, the Bible, and the kingdom of God to filter through my old unsanctified thoughts and ideas. As a result, my mind began to renew with the transformation process coming quickly and easily. Just as Paul said in his letter to the Romans, I found myself able to discern the will of God for my life. He had firmly established His ways and thoughts as He began to order my steps.

Transformation into the image of Christ is an ongoing process. Therefore, to stay on course with the renewing of our minds, we must develop strategies of humility. Remember, it is our responsibility to humble ourselves. We will constantly deal with old mindsets as He transforms us from glory to glory.

2 Corinthians 3:17-18 Now the Lord is the Spirit; and where the Spirit of the Lord is, there is liberty. ¹⁸ But we all, unveiled face, beholding as in a mirror the glory of the Lord, are being transformed into the same image from glory to glory, just as by the Spirit of the Lord.

It is important to understand that some of our old mindsets are strongholds of thinking because they are the only way we have known to think since the days of our youth. They are strongholds of thinking we must tear down for God's divine nature to take over. Again, humility and admitting to ourselves and others that we were wrong in our thought processes is the beginning of the process. We must tear down our old mindsets so that our new thought processes can take hold by being brought into captivity through obedience. As we humble ourselves, we demolish the old thought patterns.

2 Corinthians 10:4-6 *For the weapons of our warfare are not carnal but mighty in God for pulling down strongholds, ⁵* **casting down arguments and every high thing that exalts itself against the knowledge of God, bringing every thought into captivity to the obedience of Christ,** *⁶ and being ready to punish all disobedience when your obedience is fulfilled.*

As we continually trust in the Lord with all our hearts while not leaning on our understanding, God can direct our paths into all the heavenly treasures He desires to pour into our lives. As we meditate and contemplate all His precepts, they get ingrained in our hearts. When His principles get ingrained into us, the transformation process continually molds and shapes us like David and others, allowing the Heavenly Father to shape their lives according to His will and purpose.

Psalm 119:15 I will meditate on Your precepts and contemplate Your ways.

Prayer

Heavenly Father, help me focus on You as I commit my ways and thoughts to You. Allow Your Word to wash over me as Your Holy Spirit reveals Your thoughts and ways.

Devotional Poem: Lost in Thought

Lost in thought, I turn to You, oh Lord, for reflection.
In You, the mind fills with thoughts to be explored.
You are the One who turns thoughts into direction.

Committed to Your ways, Your thoughts take hold.
As destiny defines, we delight in Your affection.

Lost in thought, I delight myself in You, oh Lord.
Delighting in You, the desires of my heart are met.
Your desires becoming mine, I make right choices.
With Your desires, I'm led with a new mindset.
Standing in agreement, destiny fulfills as I rejoice.

Lost in thought, I trust You, oh Lord, for furtherance.
Trusting, I feed on Your faithfulness, no longer stalled.
Feeding on Your faithfulness, faith arises in accordance.
With faith arising, I go forth into destiny, now called.
With vision and purpose filling, I stand in concurrence.

Lost in thought, I commit my ways to You, oh Lord.
Trusting and committing, Your ways come to fruition.
As Your righteousness shines through, others are inspired.
Led into Your paths, they embrace purpose and vision.
Turning to You in all things, they, too, are stirred.

Scriptures to Meditate Upon

2 Peter 1:1-3, Colossians 1:13-14, Proverbs 16:3,9, Psalm 37:3-6. Romans 8:6-7, 1 Corinthians 2:9-16, John 14:26, Hebrews 4:12, Psalm 119:105.

~

May the Lord bless you richly as His thoughts and ways fill your mind. May your mind be renewed with His divine nature as you go forth in destiny and purpose.

Day 25

The Fragrance of Christ

2 Corinthians 2:14-15 Now be thanks unto God who always leads us in triumph in Christ, and through us diffuses the fragrance of His knowledge in every place. ⁱ⁵ For we are to God the fragrance of Christ among those who are being saved and among those who are perishing.

We live in a world contaminated by sin. Because sin is so rampant in our world today, the stench that comes from it is putrefying every stratum of our societies. The problem is that sin has become so rampant and acceptable that our senses have grown dull. Even in Christendom, the putrefaction of sin is rampant. What has happened worldwide has spilled into the Church of Jesus Christ.

In the natural, when living with certain smells, whether good or bad, our senses are dulled as they get used to them. As we step away and get a breath of fresh air and then come back, our senses become reminded of how foul the odor is. In the spiritual realm, our senses get distorted and become accustomed to sinful behavior with the inundation of corrupt values that no longer adhere to principles found in God's Word. It's time for God's people to step away to get a breath of fresh air by allowing the Holy Spirit to breathe upon them with a fresh anointing from the purity of His word. We need the Lord's fragrance to wash over us and spill into the world rather than the foulness of sinful behavior.

Notice the above passage that says we are to be a fragrance to those who are being saved (new believers) and those who perish. We are salt and light to one another and those in the world dying in their sins. As we spread Christ's fragrance everywhere, the earth fills with His fragrance rather than the stench arising from sin. Paul exhorted young Timothy to be an example of believers in all things. He said, *"Let no one despise your youth, but be an example to the believers in word, conduct, in love, in spirit, in faith, in purity."*

The Fragrance of the Lord – Treasures from Above

All the areas mentioned by Paul in his letter to Timothy bring forth the Lord's fragrance in our lives. Think about how the words of our mouths affect those around us. As James says in his epistle, *"Out of the same mouth proceed blessing and cursing. My brethren, these things ought not to be so."* Using negative words and such to tear down ideas and thoughts that are not in alignment with ours is something we encounter daily, especially with the advent of social media—Christians sparring with one another and with unbelievers over matters that only provoke contempt. This kind of sparring only adds to noxious odors rather than the fragrance of Christ.

Love, conduct, purity, and faith are what produce Christ's fragrance in our lives. Unfortunately, it seems in today's Christianity, professing Christians are just as bound up in sexual impurity and conduct as unbelievers are. In many cases, our mouths are just as foul as those in the world. These things ought not to be. As Peter said in his second epistle, we must make every effort to add virtue, knowledge, self-control, perseverance, godliness, brotherly kindness, and love to our faith. He says if we do these things, we will be fruitful in the knowledge of our Lord Jesus Christ. As we give ourselves to godliness in all areas is what helps to produce the fragrance of the Lord in all places.

Let us determine in our hearts to spread the fragrance of Christ everywhere we go rather than giving in to the stench of our times.

Prayer

Heavenly Father, I offer myself to You as a sweet-smelling sacrifice as I go forth as a vessel unto honor, who desires to leave Your fragrance everywhere I go. Help me be disciplined and full of self-control in all that I do.

Poem: The Fragrance of Christ

Before sin, in the garden, pleasant fragrances filled everywhere.
Like sweet incense, fruits, flowers, trees, and plants filled the air.
Until sin's entrance, the aroma of God's presence was relished.

Distorted by sin, foul odors wreaked, emanating effusively.
Inundated with flagrant pervasiveness, foulness endangers.

From polluted minds, rising stench renders hatred capturing.
Impurity usurping and spreading needs fragrance recapturing.
As pollution exceeds, havoc and turmoil wreak everywhere.
Evil schemes and hatred spreading, many stumble, terrorized.
With distorted senses, true fragrance is no longer recognized.

As uncleanness fills throughout, Satan's stench is everywhere.
Where are the intercessors crying for filth to be removed?
Where are the preachers calling for repentance proved?
Where are the saints of God fed up with swimming in sewers?
Now's the time to call on God to cleanse from all impurities.

As saints arise to diffuse, the Lord's fragrance fills all.
Making no provision for the flesh, His fragrance releases.
With minds renewed by His Word, His nature fills all.
As freshness fills the senses, spiritual fruit refreshes.
As sweet odors fill, love, joy, peace, and patience overflow.

As His hands and feet, the world fills with sweet fragrance.
Walking as He walked, a sweet aroma purifies the airwaves.
Cultures on the verge of ruination receive an aroma that staves.
Filling all in all with God's presence, fragrance is detected.
Joining together with one purpose, His fragrance is injected.

Scriptures to Meditate Upon

Ephesians 1:22-23, Romans 12:1-2, Acts 3:19, Galatians 5:22-25, Romans 13:14, 2 Corinthians 10:6, Ephesians 4:1-4, 1 Timothy 4:12, James 3:10, 2 Peter 1:5-11.

~

May the blessing of God be with you as you go forth into your harvest fields, spreading the fragrance of Christ everywhere.

2 Corinthians 2:14 *Now, thanks be to God who always leads us in triumph in Christ, and through us diffuses the fragrance of His knowledge in every place.*

Day 26
Truth and Error

Psalm 12:6 *The words of the Lord are pure words, like silver tried in a furnace of earth, purified seven times.*

In the One Year Devotional Bible, Niki Gumbel is quoted as saying in one of the devotionals, *"After much discussion, debate, and research, the Oxford dictionaries word of the year for 2016 was post-truth. It had shown a 2000% increase in usage during the year, spiking during the Brexit and US Presidential debates. In a 'post-truth' era, objective facts appear less influential than appeals to emotion. There is a tolerance for dishonest, inaccurate allegations and outright denial of facts. Blatant lies become routine."*

Besides Jesus, the greatest treasure from above is the truth of God's word. Biblical truth was the key to all of King David's successes. His testimony was, *"I rejoice at Your word as one who finds great treasure."* David's hope was in the Word because he realized the entirety of God's word is truth. When we fail to acknowledge God's word as truth, truth then becomes nonexistent giving birth to blatant lies — everyone believing and doing what is right in their own eyes rather than byGod who is the author of all truth. To not accept all Scripture as divinely inspired by God is error, which leads to the destruction of or cultures. Therefore, we must believe and walk in the Truth of God's Holy word, if we are to penetrate the lies of Satan, who is incapable of standing in truth.

Truth is one of the most powerful weapons we possess as Christians. When we walk in the truth of God's word, Satan's ploys and darts will not affect us. Amid truth, Satan has nowhere to stand. Jesus spoke of this when he addressed the Pharisees because of their hypocrisy.

John 8:43-44 *"Why do you not understand My speech? Because you are not able to listen to My word. ⁴⁴ You are of your father the devil, and the* *desires of your father you want to do. He was a murderer from the beginning and **does not stand in the truth because there is no truth in him**. When he speaks a lie, he speaks from his own resources, for he is a liar and the father of it."*

When we speak and walk in the truth of God's word, we pull the rug out from under Satan's feet and throw him off balance as he hurls his darts toward us. He can't hurt us because the truth protects us. His darts hit the target only when we give in to his lies. The belt of truth is our weapon against all his lies and deceit.

When we believe in Jesus Christ and submit to His Lordship, the truth of God's holy word enters our lives. By submitting to His Lordship, we make a conscious decision to believe that God inspired all Scripture. Even though we may not understand everything in His word, we accept it as His purified word for us to be complete and thoroughly equipped.

2 Timothy 3:16-17 *All Scripture is given by inspiration of God and is profitable for doctrine, for reproof, for correction, for instruction in righteousness, [17] that the man of God may be thoroughly equipped for every good work.*

False truth and error come into play when our opinions and ideas get exalted above the Word. We are in error when we disagree with God's word or let our emotions dictate our beliefs about a particular issue. We don't have the right to pick and choose which Scriptures are divinely inspired or which are not. Instead, we must align ourselves with the entirety of God's word, just as David did.

Psalm 119:159-160 *Consider how I love Your precepts; revive me according to Your lovingkindness. [160] The entirety of Your word is truth, and every one of Your righteous judgments endures forever.*

Many in the Church end up in error due to a lack of belief in the entirety of God's word. There are many false teachers and prophets in the Church who compromise or water God's word down for the sake of relevancy, giving Satan a foothold to set his false prophets and teachers in place. One of his greatest ploys is mixing a little truth with lies and deceit, which he did with Eve and when Satan tempted Jesus in with wilderness. He mixed truth with his lies. Jesus defeated Satan because He knew the Word of God in its entirety.

Today, many of God's people are Bible illiterate because they have not taken the time to immerse themselves in His word. As a result, they have no idea when biting into the enemy's lies. Instead, what they taste seems good to their natural senses, as the forbidden fruit bit into by Adam and Eve did.

If we are to discern the difference between truth and error, we must put on the whole armor of God, especially the belt of truth, so that the Church will be the pillar and ground of all truth. Truth must emanate from the Church so Satan has nowhere to stand amid the world's nations. It begins with each of us walking in the truth of God's word rather than following those who compromise and water it down. Then, God will cleanse His Church from Satan's trickery as it is washed in the water of His Word by adhering to its entirety.

As we commit to partake of this great treasure of God's truth we will be adequately equipped for whatever lies and half-truths the enemy throws our way. Therefore, we must allow God to weave His truth in its entirety into the fiber of our beings. In doing so, we will save ourselves and those around us. Paul wrote to young Timothy, *"Give attention to reading, exhortation, doctrine, meditate on these things; give yourself entirely to them, that your progress may be evident to all. Take heed to yourself and the doctrine.* **Continue in them, for in doing this, you will save yourself and those who hear you."**

Prayer

Father, I open my heart to you and permit you to wash me thoroughly with the washing of water that comes from giving myself to studying and meditating upon Your Word.

Devotional Poem: Battle for Truth

No longer relevant, the Church cries in disbelief.
Pleasing whims of others, she stands without voice.
No longer preaching sound doctrine, she's intimidated.
Compromising truth for relevancy, the enemy laughs.
Caught in a web of deceit, she cries for relief.

Without truth, Satan comes carrying out ploys.
With lies, itching ears give ear to his voice.

Truth and Error – Treasures from Above

Giving ear, they do what's right in their own eyes.
Laughing, he fills the vacuum the Church abdicates.
Marching forward in lies, multitudes join in war cries.

Forsaking truth, like Pharisees of old, error comes into play.
Illiterate in Scripture, the anointing no longer profits.
Falling into Satan's schemes, they wrested for what benefits.
Fearing controversy, diluting truth, they give heed to false ways.
Paving the way for the antichrist spirit, they stand disconcerted.

Now's the time to strap on the belt of truth and armor of light.
Now's the time for Bride's voice to call for truth valiantly.
Now's the time for the remnant to lead with ferocity and might.
Now's the time for apostles and prophets to speak boldly.
Now's the time to draw together with one voice, collectively.

Speaking forcibly, the Church a pillar of truth, outnumbers.
Standing against truth, nowhere to stand, Satan blunders.
Lies and deceit known to all, his ploys quickly dispel.
Deceiving spirits crying fervently, the Church easily quells.
Multitudes who embraced lies now cry for truth to excel.

Truth in play, hell's gates give way as Jesus builds His Church.
Purposing to be a part of all Jesus is doing, forward we march.
Joining together in unity, the enemy's voice is easily quelled.
As glory rises upon us, we bask in His love and power.
God Omnipotent reigning, nothing's too difficult in this hour.

Scriptures to Meditate Upon

Psalm 119:147,160-162, Colossians 2:8, Matthew 22:29, Ephesians 6:14, Romans 13:12, Matthew 16:18, 2 Corinthians 10:4-6, Matthew 4:1-11, Ephesians 5:26, 1 Timothy 4:13-16.

~

May God bless you richly as you open the treasures that pour forth from His word to you. You'll be blessed beyond measure.

Day 27
Flames of Fire

Psalm 104:3-4 *He lays the beams of His upper chambers in the waters, who makes His clouds His chariot, who walks on the wings of the wind, who makes His angels spirits, His ministers a flame of fire.*

The Father's only begotten Son is the greatest treasure we have from above, who came to give us salvation that brought us into fellowship with the Father, Son, and Holy Spirit. He came to reveal the Father in all His glory by showing us how great salvation is. As Peter mentions in his first epistle, it's something the prophets and the angels of God desired to partake of but couldn't. We, however, have been blessed beyond measure as recipients of all that God has planned and proposed for humankind.

Jesus came in the fullness of time to fulfill the Father's prophetic purpose. The prophet Isaiah spoke of this when he prophesied a Son would be given, called Wonderful, Counselor, Mighty God, Everlasting God, and Prince of Peace.[17] Because the fullness of the Godhead rests upon Him, the Father gave His son names that represent His fullness.[18] God, in His zeal and sovereignty, brought forth the fulfillment of Isaiah's remarkable prophecy. For every prophetic purpose, His Holy prophets have spoken through the ages; God continues to fulfill through His zeal.

Before Jesus can return to earth to set up His throne as it is in Heaven, everything that His holy prophets have spoken must be fulfilled with the restoration of all things being complete. Peter spoke of this in his message after the healing of the lame man at Solomon's Portico.

---

[17] Isaiah 9:6
[18] Colossians 2:9

Flames of Fire – Treasures from Above

Acts 3:19 "Repent therefore and be converted, that your sins may be blotted out, so that times of refreshing may come from the presence of the Lord, [20] and that He may send Jesus Christ who was preached to you before, [21] **whom heaven must receive (retain) until the times of restoration of all things, which God had spoken by the mouth of His Holy prophets since the world began."**

Peter and the others were baptized with the Holy Spirit and fire the Day God fully fulfilled the Feast of Pentecost, just as God fulfilled the Feast of Passover by Jesus, the perfect Lamb of God. Then, filled with the power of the Holy Spirit, these disciples went forth like flames of fire, just as the prophet Joel prophesied, fulfilling the prophetic purposes of God for their generation. The opening passage on the previous page explains how God brings His prophetic purposes to pass in His sovereignty. He makes His angels spirits and His ministers flames of fire.

We find this true as we study the lives of these early disciples and apostles of Christ throughout the New Testament. When it came time to fulfill the prophecy of Joel, God sent a mighty rushing wind to baptize them in the Holy Spirit. The Holy Spirit came to them with tongues of fire, transforming them into flames of fire as they went forth, fulfilling the Father's prophetic purposes. Just as God transformed these early disciples into flames of fire, He can do the same for us.

When it came time to fulfill the prophecies of the Gentiles coming into this great salvation, God orchestrated the event by giving a Gentile non-believer, Cornelius, and a Jewish believer, Peter, visions that brought them together to fulfill this prophetic purpose. Of course, like flames of fire, both Cornelius and Peter had to obey the visions they had received. But it was God, in His zeal, who made it happen. The example of Cornelius and Peter is a beautiful example of how God's sovereignty and our free will meet together to fulfill prophetic purposes. We also see how God used angels to bring forth His prophetic purposes in both the lives of Peter and Paul.

As we approach the end of the age, there are many prophetic purposes God must yet fulfill with His flames of fire before He releases Jesus from Heaven. God is preparing His vessels of honor, who will go forth like flames of fire with their passion ignited to fulfill all His Holy prophets have prophesied concerning the end of the age.

Will you be a prepared vessel of honor with the proper amount of oil in your lamp to be ignited, or will you be found sleeping when the Holy Spirit comes upon us like a mighty rushing wind as He did with the early disciples? The choice is yours to make. Now is the time for His bride to make herself ready. When God decides to move suddenly, it comes without notice.

Prayer

Heavenly Father, I commit my heart to you. Make me one of Your ministers as a flame of fire, fulfilling Your prophetic purposes.

Poem: Wings of the Wind, Flames of Fire

Coming on wings of the wind, He fills our vessels.
The clouds His chariot, He comes setting us aflame.
In rushing winds, He comes with tongues of fire to ignite.
Filled with flaming fire, His vessels go forth in His Name.
In great expectancy, His name is proclaimed with might.

Passion ignited, transforming power produces purity.
Chaff beginning to burn, the old disappears into ashes.
Gentle breezes blowing, newness comes with surety.
In each new day, there's expectation of what's ahead.
Chaff continuing to burn, old strongholds disintegrate.

Made anew by His Spirit, vision, and purpose awaken.
Divine abilities and gifts birthed, He gives sail to the wind.
Flames igniting in explosive power, He gives birth to ministry.
With the mind of Christ, confidence explodes with desire.
Clothed with splendor, He makes His ministers flames of fire.

Wings of the wind breathing on dry bones, they awaken.
Performing in His zeal, The Lord fulfills what's written.
His chosen ones anointed; they go forth as flames of fire.

With explosive power, He infuses with authority on high.
With mighty winds, He gives sail to those standing by.

The bride, fully clothed in her fullness, stands fully dressed.
A chaste virgin, measured by His stature, radiates in fullness.
Wedding garments placed, she's made ready for her day, now near.
From the clouds of heaven, the Bridegroom comes to receive her.
Joined together, she's known as He's known, now consummated.

Scriptures to Meditate Upon

1 Peter 1:10-12, Isaiah 9:6-7, Acts 10:1-16, Acts 2:1-4, 1 Corinthians 5:7, Acts 5:19-20, 12-5-9, 27:22-24, Joel 2:28-29, Revelation 19:6.

~

May the blessing of the Lord be with you as you are sanctified and consecrated unto Him, who fills you with the Holy Spirit's explosive power to fulfill His purposes for this generation.

Day 28
The Potter's Wheel

Jeremiah 18:2 Arise and go down to the potter's house, and there I will cause you to hear My words.

When we come to Christ, many of us are broken and shattered vessels in need of a complete makeover. We were marred clay pieces in the Potter's hands, needed mending. We needed a do-over. Thankfully, one of the great blessings of being born again is that we become new creations in Christ, as Paul stated so clearly when he said, *"Therefore if anyone is in Christ, he is a new creation; old things have passed away, behold all things have become new."* The passage below describes this process perfectly as He places us on the Potter's wheel.

Jeremiah 18:1-6 The word which came to Jeremiah from the Lord saying: ² "Arise and go down to the potter's house, and there I will cause you to hear My words. ³ Then I went down to the potter's house, and there he was making something at the wheel. ⁴ ***And the vessel that he made of clay was marred in the hand of the Potter; so, he made it again into another vessel*** *as it seemed good to the Potter to make. ⁵ Then the word of the Lord came to me, saying: ⁶ O house of Israel, can I not do with you as this potter?" says the Lord.* **"Look, as the clay is in the Potter's hand, so are you in My hand,** *O house of Israel!"*

Our Heavenly Father, the Potter, constantly molds and shapes our lives according to the purpose He had in mind when He created us. In one of his Psalms, David said, *"My frame was not hidden from You when I was made in secret, and skillfully wrought forth in the earth's lowest parts.* ***Your eyes saw my substance, being yet unformed. And in Your book, they all were written; the days were fashioned for me when there were none."*** [19] As Father God molds and shapes our lives, His thoughts towards us are precious, and the

---
[19] Psalm 139:16

sum is excellent.

Jeremiah 29:11 *For I know the thoughts that I think toward you, says the Lord, thoughts of peace and not evil, to give you a future and a hope.*

We have all been peculiarly designed for the unique role the Father had in mind when we were yet unformed. We can, by choice, be either a piece of clay that is soft and easily moldable or a hard piece of clay that requires a hammer and chisel. When we constantly chafe at the bit through stubbornness and disobedience, the Potter takes us off the wheel, uses His hammer and chisel, and goes to work. It's a laborious process because He disciplines those He loves. Staying on the wheel as a soft piece of moldable clay involves humility and submission to the Lord's ways. God knows our beginning and end, so it's to our advantage to stay on the wheel as He continually fashions us according to His will and purpose for our lives.

The Potter allows weaknesses to surface while staying on the wheel. As hard lumps of clay come to the surface, He removes them painlessly. Sensing how He molds and shapes us according to our calling and assignments, we stay on the wheel. The more committed we are to His handiwork and giving Him free rein to mold and shape as He pleases, the more we become vessels unto honor whom He uses mightily for His purposes. As the prophet Daniels says, *"They that know their God shall be strong and carry out great exploits."*[20]

As we give ourselves to the Potter's wheel and allow His treasures from above to fill our lives, we go forth, fulfilling His purposes. We fulfill the destiny He spoke into existence that was explicitly designed for us to achieve—a destiny that was marked out when He formed us in our mother's womb.[21]

Prayer

Father, God, I commit my life to You like a piece of soft, moldable clay. Help me stay on the Potter's wheel so that I will be all You have fashioned me to be. Give me patience and understanding as You perform Your will and purpose in me.

---

[20] Daniel 11:32 NKJV
[21] Psalm 139:16-17

Poem: As the Wheel Turns

As the wheel turns, the Potter shapes for peculiarity.
With marred clay, He shapes with wisdom and clarity.
As clay in His hands, so are we as He takes pleasure.
Delighting at the wheel, He creates marvelously.
As the wheel turns, He shapes each vessel uniquely.

The wheel turning, He shapes fulfilling vision and purpose.
Accordingly, the Potter arranges His chosen vessels.
With precision, He molds and shapes for intended use.
Knowing their future, how each responds, He shapes.
The wheel turning, He molds with eternal purposes in mind.

As the wheel turns, in mercy, He allows for weaknesses.
Recognizing imperfections in all, He continues to shape.
With perfect views of their end, He shapes accordingly.
Knowing whether they are unto honor or not, He molds.
As the wheel turns, there's sadness for those who resist.

The wheel turning, not knowing the end result, we ponder.
Catching glimpses of His hands at work, we become pliable.
Carefully watching His vessels in action, the Potter smiles.
Setting up divine appointments, He chooses wisely for all.
As the wheel turns, He shapes as tasks are completed.

As the wheel turns, the chosen fully embrace their Potter,
With delight in the Potter's work, they energetically go forth.
With anticipation, pressing through obstacles, they trust.
Knowing the Potter is intimately acquainted, faith arises.
The wheel turning, fruitfulness is recognized by all.

Scriptures to Meditate Upon

2 Corinthians 5:17, Psalm 139:14-17, Psalm 32:9, James 3:3, Hebrews 12:11, James 4:6-7, 2 Timothy 2;20-21, Daniel 11:32.

~

May God bless you mightily as you stay on the Potter's wheel, carrying out great exploits for Him and His kingdom.

Day 29
Getting Into God's Playbook

John 12:26 "If anyone serves Me, let him follow Me; and where I am, there My servant will be also. If anyone serves Me, My Father will answer."

In football, players who are often written into their coach's playbook to make the big plays are those who know how to play their position well. They are where they're supposed to be when the play goes into action. They must know their position well and how to position themselves to make the great plays. When their coaches recognize their ability to make the plays consistently, they become an integral part of His playbook.

In Christ, we are all given positions, ministries, gifts, and talents that make up our calling in God. We all have parts to play in the game of life. God desires to use us according to our natural and spiritual abilities. The more committed we are to playing according to His playbook, the more opportunities we will have to make great plays. He wants to set up plays that fit the person He has uniquely fashioned us to be. Jesus alluded to this in the above Scripture, saying, *"Where I am, there My servant will also be."* Jesus says He expects us to handle the ball when given to us. Do you desire divine appointments where God visibly manifests Himself for you to work alongside Him? If so, God will set divine appointments in place for you.

Years ago, while reading a book my wife was proofing for an evangelist friend, I was amazed by the vast number of divine appointments he was having. From witnessing and leading Pro-athletes to Christ to avoiding secret service agents so he could give a prophetic word to Presidents, he had one divine encounter after another. As I pondered this, I heard the Lord whisper, "It's because he's always obedient to be where I'm working in his harvest field." Jesus said to His disciples after having a divine appointment with the woman at the well, *"Do you not say, 'There are still four months then comes the harvest'? Behold, I say, lift up your eyes and look at the fields, for they are already white for harvest!"*

God has given each of us a harvest field to work in according to the grace and natural abilities He gave us. Your harvest field is your everyday life that involves work, school, play, shopping, your neighborhood, and anything else that comes your way. As we look up to see where the Lord works, divine appointments come our way. When we are faithful to serve God in the position, He has ordained for us, He sets us up to make great plays as He recognizes our obedience and desire to be written into His playbook. The Lord is waiting for you to take your harvest field seriously. He desires to get you into His playbook by setting up some great plays designed explicitly for the gifts and talents He's given you.

Matthew 9:37-38 *Then He said to His disciples, "The harvest is plentiful, but the laborers are few. ³⁸ Therefore, pray the Lord of the harvest to send out laborers into His harvest."*

The dynamic of God is that He is always at work and involved in making plans to bring forth greater kingdom dimensions, not only in our lives but for the people, He puts in our paths. Are we sitting on the bench watching others make the plays, or are we in the game making great plays for God? Do we desire to be written into God's playbook, or are we satisfied with sitting on the bench? It is up to us! It's our choice.

Prayer

Father, I pray for wisdom from above as I enter Your harvest field. I open my eyes to see where You're already at work on my right and left. Allow the gifts and talents You gave me to be for Your glory.

Poem: The Harvest Field

Looking upward, sensing God's hand over all, we pursue.
Looking inward, we question our part in the harvest.
Looking outward, the harvest ripe stands in full view.
Looking forward, faith arises, gaining vision and purpose.
Looking backward, sensing time wasted, we woo.

Ready and willing, He shows how to labor unharnessed.
Inventory tallied, talents and gifts, He uses for harvest.
Sense of purpose rising within, we commit to Him above.
From the wisdom above, treasures given are employed.
Shown purpose for all given, fruit comes forth unspoiled.

Into His field, eyes wide open to those around us, we see.
Pain and turmoil on faces encountered, we labor to free.
Taking note, hopelessness rests on many walking aimlessly.
Hoping for help, those hungry stand with signs shamelessly.
Fields white for harvest, we pray for more laborers.

Dying to self, embracing His cross, purpose fulfills.
Seeing needs before us, we ask, "What would Jesus do?"
No longer questioning motives, we to trust in His guidance.
Committing ways to Him, He directs and chooses in alliance.
In obedience and faithfulness, forward we go into His harvest.

~

Scriptures to Meditate Upon

1 Corinthians 12:4-11, Ephesians 4:7, Romans 12:3-8, 1 Peter 4:10, John 4:35, Proverbs 16:3, 9.

May the blessing of the Lord be with you as you go forth into your harvest field today. May your eyes be open to all that comes your way.

Day 30
Great Lovers of God

Matthew 22:36-38 "Teacher, which is the great commandment in the law?" Jesus said to him, " 'You shall love the LORD your God with all your heart, with all your soul, and with all your mind.' "This is the first and great commandment."

Have you ever thought about or even desired to become a great lover of God? To be a great lover of God should be something every born-again Christian contemplates. We know that God so loved the world that He gave His only begotten Son so we may have eternal life. Because of God's great love toward us, we are not only forgiven and granted entrance into His kingdom but also given an abundance of daily blessings that continually flow our way from His storehouse of precious treasures. The Holy Spirit of God gives us everything we need as we go forth in His love.

***Psalm 68:19** Blessed be the Lord, who daily loads us with benefits, the God of our salvation.*

What is it that the Father expects from us? How do we appreciate all He's given from His great treasures? In His Word, we find all He desires from us is to become great lovers of Him. Because He first loved us when we were still in our sins, we are to love Him. So, with love as an action word, what actions express our Love towards Him? What is it that makes us great lovers of God? The answer is simple. It is found in the first and great commandment.

***Luke 10:27** So he answered and said, "You shall love the Lord your God with all your heart, with all your soul, with all your strength, and with all your mind, and your neighbor as yourself."*

Jesus mentions five action items in these passages of Scripture. We are to love the Lord with all our heart, soul, strength, and mind and love our neighbors as much as we love ourselves. These five actions include every area of our lives. He wants us to give our lives in exchange for what He has given us. We now belong to Him because He bought and paid for us with His precious blood.

You shall love the Lord your God:

- With all your heart – the emotional nature
- With all your soul – the willing nature
- With all your strength – the physical nature
- With all your mind – the intellectual nature

The total person loves God – mind, will, emotion, and strength. We are all strong in some areas while weak in others. If we fail to love God in each area equally, we will become unbalanced in our love toward God. It will also show up in our relationships with the people God put in our lives.

For example, if you love God with a strength of mind and a weakness of emotion, you will become an intellectualist with a legalistic approach to God and others.

If you love Him with a strength of emotion and weakness of mind, you will be a sentimentalist in religion, governed by your feelings, expressed in excess of affection or sentiment.

If you love Him with a strength of will and a weakness of emotion, you will be a man of iron who is not very approachable.

When we love God with all our strength of emotion, will, mind, and physical strength, we will have a balanced strength of character that genuinely loves God as He has commanded us.

Therefore, let us look at these areas and see how God wants us to love Him with all our heart, soul, mind, and strength. When we love God in each area, we also fulfill the command to love our neighbor as we love ourselves.

Loving God with all our hearts comes through an appreciation of genuinely embracing His forgiveness. As we grow in the Lord, it comes through worship and praise while continually adoring Him. The story of the sinful woman, who, in her love and devotion towards Christ, threw herself at Him and began to wash His feet with her tears is a beautiful picture of loving God with the strength of emotion and heart. She was not afraid to lose her dignity in Christ's presence.

How many of us often find ourselves, like the Pharisees in Christ's presence, aloof and disengaged while playing intellectual games with Him? Yet, as we seek to spend time in personal worship of Him, the hardness of our hearts melts away so that we love Him through our emotions.

To love God with our soul represents a willingness to obey and follow Him in what He has purposed for our lives. It involves training our souls to submit to those areas that resist His rule. Paul spoke of the need to discipline his body.[22] Likewise, David cried out for His soul to submit to God. So often, we may think we are doing good in our relationship with God, only to realize after succumbing to temptations, we lack the discipline that comes from training our souls to submit. We must discipline those unruly areas if we love God with all our souls.

To love the Lord with our mind represents a love for His word. Mary, the sister of Lazarus, is a perfect example of this as she sought a deeper life with Christ. Her devotion and love for Christ caused her to want to sit at His feet and hear His word. Her heart was consumed with a desire to fill her mind with His word. We see a picture of Mary loving Jesus with heartfelt warmth, passion, and love for His word. As a young Christian, the first prophecy I received from the Lord was that my love for God's word would bring me into intimacy with Him. I still find this true after 48 years of walking with the Lord.

Loving God with all our strength implies dedicating and sacrificing the strength of our bodies to Him for His cause and purposes. You are willing to go out of your way to help others by laying down your life. You esteem their needs as being more important than yours.

1 John 3:16 By this, we know love because He laid down His life for us. And we also ought to lay down our lives for the brethren.

---

[22] 1 Corinthians 9:27

Romans 12:1 *I beseech you therefore, brethren, by the mercies of God, that you present your bodies a living sacrifice, holy, acceptable to God, which is your reasonable service.*

As you can see, being a great lover of God involves giving Him the best you have to offer, including your heart, soul, mind, and strength. So give God your best, and He will bless you beyond measure.

Prayer

Father, I come to You today, giving You my heart, soul, mind, and strength so that You can work Your will and purpose in me so that I may become a great Lover of You.

Poem: Becoming a Great Lover of God

Caught whirlwinds of self-glory, God breaks through.
Looking beyond our sin, His love gives hope to all.
Filled with love in abundance, He draws unto Himself.
From His great treasures, He provides things needed.
Love breaking through, desires to give bring forth.

Desiring to be great lovers of Him, we question.
What do we do for Him, who fills with such great love?
Like flashes of light in the night, His Word conveys.
Loving with heart, strength, mind, and soul, we obey.
Loving neighbors, we fulfill His great commandment.

Loving emotionally, we give in praise, and worship.
Bowing before Him filled with praise; we adore Him.
No longer playing intellectual games, we worship.
With hearts engaged, we go pursuing His desires.
Losing dignity before Him, we become fools for Christ.

With strength, we present our bodies as living sacrifices.
Giving sacrificially, His body refreshes and strengthens.
Esteeming others more important; we give sacrificially.
Knowing our reasonable service, we give of ourselves.
Girding loins of our minds, we rest our hope on grace.

Willingly submitting our souls, we give to His desires.
Embracing discipline, we train our souls by His Spirit.
Obediently giving free rein, He accesses areas stumbling.
Confronting the will, we embrace bitter herbs transforming.
Reigned in, we go into battle, fully engaged in His love.

Minds filled with His Word, we press for revelation.
Pressing in love in His Word, He revives daily.
Morning dawn rising, we meditate in His Word.
Holding His word before us, we refrain from all evil.
His Word hidden in our hearts, we keep from sinning.

Giving praise and honor to Him above, we give thanks.
With His great love taking root, we become conquerors.
Becoming His great lovers, He fills with abundance.
Fulfilling His great commandment, destiny takes over.
Treasures pouring forth from above, we're content.

Scriptures to Meditate Upon

John 3:16, 1 Peter 1:3-5, 2 Peter 1:2-4, Romans 5:8, 1 John 4:19, Luke 7:36-38, Luke 10:38-42, Psalm 119:140, Philippians 2:4.

~

May the riches of His blessings be loaded upon you daily as you become a great lover of God by obeying the first and great commandment to love the Lord with all your heart, soul, mind, and strength.

Day 31
Come Holy Spirit

John 16:7 *"Nevertheless, I tell you the truth. It is to your advantage that I go away; for if I do not go away, the Helper will not come to you, but if I depart, I will send Him to you."*

The Father has given us two beautiful gifts which enable us to experience all that flows from His great treasures. They are His word and the Holy Spirit. These two gifts are the keys to all He desires to pour into our lives.

During the Last Supper, after Judas departed to betray Him, Jesus had a meaningful conversation with His disciples that immensely affected their lives and ours. He began telling them how important the Holy Spirit's coming would be to them. With the promise of the Holy Spirit coming to take His place, He told them it was to their advantage for Him to go away; otherwise, the Holy Spirit would not come. In the conversation, John writes in his gospel concerning what Jesus had to say about how the coming of the Holy Spirit would affect our lives. First, he defined why it would be advantageous for Him to come into our lives. Then, he explained how it would benefit all who call upon Him.

When we receive the revelation of the benefits of the Holy Spirit as our helper, the prayer of our hearts should be, ***"Come, Holy Spirit."***

He comes as our helper. Jesus spoke of the Holy Spirit coming to be our helper. Think about the many ways you have had someone come alongside you at various times and give you a helping hand in a difficult task. What a relief it was to make your life more manageable! We have a helper on call 24-7 to make our lives more viable. Unfortunately, we sometimes put the Holy Spirit in a box, limiting Him to spiritual things. We are encouraged in Proverbs to acknowledge the Lord in all our ways, not just some of our ways. Our part is to recognize Him as our helper in everything we do, saying, "Come Holy Spirit and be the helper of my joy."

John 14:16-17a "And I will pray the Father, and He will give you another Helper that He may abide with you forever—the Spirit of truth."

He comes as our teacher. We have the most outstanding teacher in the universe at our disposal. Yet, so many of us are unlearned in the ways of the Lord. The Holy Spirit has come to teach us everything pertaining to life and godliness. We must remember that God is intimately acquainted with all our ways. Because He created and designed us according to His plans and purposes, He knows how to teach us in ways we can fully understand and comprehend. As we pray, "Come Holy Spirit," He will teach us whatever we require. All we have to do is say, ***"Come Holy Spirit and teach me."***

John 14:26 "But the Helper, the Holy Spirit, whom the Father will send in My name, He will teach you all things, and bring into remembrance all the things I said to you."

He comes to give us victory over sin. When John the Baptist prophesied the coming of the Holy Spirit, He said Jesus would baptize us with the Holy Spirit and fire to purge our sins and hurtful ways. Because we have the same Spirit that raised Christ from the dead, He will give life to our mortal bodies. He has made us more than conquerors in all things by leading us in triumph over the sins that wage against our souls. Those who walk in the Spirit will not fulfill the lusts of the flesh. All we must do is say, ***"Come, Holy Spirit, help me to lay aside the sins that so easily ensnare me."***

Matthew 3:11-12 "I indeed baptize you with water unto repentance, but He who is coming after me is mightier than I, whose sandals I am not worthy to carry. He will baptize you with the Holy Spirit and fire. [12] His winnowing fan is in His hand, and He will thoroughly clean out His threshing floor and gather His wheat into the barn, but He will burn up the chaff with unquenchable fire."

He comes to bring us peace. Jesus also spoke of how the Holy Spirit would continually bring peace into our lives no matter what circumstances we are going through. Just as Jesus calmed the storms on more than one occasion for His disciples, the Holy Spirit is there to calm the storms in our lives. All we must do is say, ***"Come Holy Spirit and give me the peace that will calm the storms of my life."***

John 14:27 *"Peace I leave with you, My peace I give to you; not as the world gives do, I give to you. Let not your heart be troubled, neither let it be afraid."*

He comes as our guide. As we journey through the many seasons of our lives, we must make decisions that will ultimately affect the direction we are going in. We desperately need a guide to give us the wisdom to make the right choices. Thankfully, we have a God-given Guide who knows everything and continually searches the Father's heart concerning our lives. He gives us wisdom and guidance as we look toward the future. All we must do is say, ***"Come Holy Spirit, be my guide."***

John 16:13-15 *"However, when He, the Spirit of truth, has come, He will guide you into all truth; for He will not speak on His own authority, but whatever He hears He will speak, and He will tell you things to come.* ^{14} *He will glorify Me, for He will take of what is mine and declare it to you.* ^{15} *All things that the Father has are Mine; therefore, I said He will take Mine and declare it to you."*

He comes to empower us. Before His ascension into heaven, Jesus promised His disciples that the Holy Spirit would come with explosive power, giving them the same anointing the Father gave Him. As a result, they could do the same mighty works He had been doing during His three and one-half years of ministry.

Acts 1:8 *"But you shall receive power when the Holy Spirit has come upon you, and you shall be witnesses to Me in Jerusalem and Samaria, and in all the world, and to the end of the earth.*

With all the Holy Spirit pouring into our lives, we have much to be thankful for as He continually fills us with His anointing. The question is, "Are we taking full advantage of all that we have at our disposal, or are we missing out because we're not crying out daily, ***'Come Holy Spirit and empower me to go forth using the gifts and the anointing You've given?'"***

Prayer

Heavenly Father, I humbly come to You today, asking You to fill my heart with Your fullness. Forgive me for not taking full advantage of all You have sent the Holy Spirit to do in my life. Open my ears to hear all He desires to declare unto me as I pray, *"Come, Holy Spirit."*

Poem: Come Holy Spirit

The Holy Spirit, accessible to all, comes with power.
In His Spirit, He comes to all with tongues of fire.
Now available, promises given come to all called.
From Your Spirit, living water flows to all enthralled.
Giving the Holy Spirit, the Father delights in all called.

Come, Holy Spirit, as we seek and ask for your presence.
Asking in faith, believing, we come with expectations.
Seeking with whole hearts, He fills with excellence.
From His Spirit, new languages come with conviction.
With living water, He fills with prophetic anticipation.

Come Holy Spirit, burn chaff that holds back purity.
With fires burning, comes conviction that possesses.
Repenting, He refreshes, quickened to walk in morality.
Hurtful ways shown holding back, we acquiesce.
No longer hindered, we press to obtain full access.

Come, Holy Spirit, guide as we walk in Your ways.
Leading in righteousness, lead with Your desires.
In conformity to Your image, lead as we gaze.
As we follow, lead away from Satan's tempting fires.
Help us to know how powerful we are in Your ways.

Come Holy Spirit, teach the ways of the Father, so fine.
With anointing, teach all pertaining to life while dining.
Teaching to number days, we're given to Your ways.
In all given, reveal all that's in Your heart of hearts.
Dripping as dew, Your doctrine declares and imparts.

Come Holy Spirit, release gifts to encourage and build.
Release healing and miracles to heal as Jesus did.
As the prophetic unfolds, reveal the Father's intentions.
With the gift of tongues, release mysteries in the Spirit.
With discerning of spirits, reveal the enemy's pretensions.

Giving thanks to Him who gave, we delight in His works.
Giving glory to Jesus, we praise Him for what's offered.

Scriptures to Meditate Upon

John 7:37-39, Luke 11:9-13, Proverbs 3:6, 1 John 2:20, 27, Psalm 139:3, 14, Hebrews 12:1, Romans 8:5-11, 2 Corinthians 2:14, Romans 8:37, Philippians 4:6-7, 1 Corinthians 2:10-16, 1 Corinthians 12:7, Ephesians 1:17-18.

~

May the Lord bless you richly as the Holy Spirit infuses your life with His divine nature bringing you into all that God has purposed for your life.

Day 32
Stop and Listen!

2 Timothy 2:24-26 And the servant of the Lord must not quarrel but be gentle to all, able to teach, patient, ^{25} in humility correcting those who are in opposition, if God perhaps will grant them repentance, so that they may know the truth, ^{26} and that they may come to their senses and escape the snare of the devil, having been taken captive by him to do his will.

If there was ever a time to stop and listen, now is as good as any time. Today, our world is being turned upside down, with righteousness called evil, while evil is called good. So, writing to Timothy, Paul's son in the faith, he wrote, *"In the last days perilous times will come: For men will be lovers of themselves, lovers of money, boasters, proud, blasphemers, disobedient to parents, unthankful, unholy, unloving, unforgiving, slanderers, without self-control, brutal, despisers of good, traitors, headstrong, haughty, lovers of pleasure rather than lovers of God, and having a form of godliness but denying the power."*

Paul's description of the end-time environment adequately describes our present-day environment. The question for us as godly Christians is, how do we respond in love to such a hostile environment? Wasn't it Jesus who said, *"Love your enemies?"*

As Jesus often entered into dialogue with those who opposed Him with questions designed to trap Him, His reply was, "Have you not read?" When speaking to His disciples, He often encouraged them to listen with their hearts. There were also times when His discussions ended with, *"He who has ears to hear, let him hear."* He would often teach with parables so that only those who had ears trained to hear the Father's voice could listen to.

Jesus continually relied on wisdom from above when dealing with opposing views and voices. He took the time to stop and listen. There are various interpretations of what Jesus wrote on the ground when confronted with the woman caught in adultery. Could it have been something as simple as stopping to listen for the wisdom from His Father above while doodling on the ground? He made a point of saying, at various times, that He only does what He sees the Father doing. His life exemplified the characteristic of taking the time to stop and listen before engaging with His enemies.

What Jesus is saying to all of us is if we are to hear through our spirits, we must first take the time to stop and listen. So often, we speak from emotional or political perspectives instead of the reality of what His Word has to say. As a result, we find ourselves caught in the rhetoric of the day, speaking unkind and hurtful things. We should stop and listen before we parrot what we are hearing from ungodly sources. Stopping and listening gives us time to examine our hearts and minds before saying anything. When speaking the truth, we must speak out of a spirit of genuine love toward those we are addressing. Without love, we're just noisy gongs. Paul gives some good advice regarding opposing views in the opening passage of Scripture.

Our goal should not be to win arguments while losing opportunities to win souls. As Paul said, we must be gentle and patient with those who oppose us.[23] We should always take the time to stop and listen before engaging those with different perspectives; otherwise, we will fall into Satan's ploys. God will give us the wisdom needed for each situation from above, just as He did for Jesus. We have the mind of Christ.

James 3:17-18 *But the wisdom that is from above is first pure, then peaceable, gentle, willing to yield, full of mercy and good fruits, without partiality and hypocrisy.* ^{18} *Now, the fruit of righteousness is sown in peace by those who make peace.*

As Christians, God has called us to be peacemakers. As Jesus said, *"Blessed are the peacemakers."* Amid all the rhetoric in our polarized societies, we are needed as peacemakers who can diffuse situations with our calm and gentle ways so that the glory of God can shine through hate-filled environments. Let the fruit of

---

[23] 2 Timothy 2:23-26

righteousness come forth by those who make for peace. Let us all stop and listen to the voice of the Holy Spirit. Let us be the voices of reason amid our world's turmoil. People are crying out for release from the snares of the enemy. Let us gird up the loins of our minds as we feed upon God's Word. Let us not be like those to whom Jesus questioned, "Have you not read?"

Prayer

Father, I come to You asking for wisdom from above to help me be gentle and kind towards those who may oppose me. Help me be a peacemaker in all situations so that Your glory will shine through. I pray that those I encounter who do not know You will have seeds planted in their hearts through Your love and kindness that pours through me.

Poem: Cries in the Wind

Cries in the wind, we hear all that's not right.
Hate destroying, we hear cries in the night.
Undistinguishable, right from wrong, mayhem rules.
Everyone right in their own eyes, frustration exceeds.
Hate and violence spewing, sadness supersedes.

Cries in the wind, we hear stop and listen.
Giving way to frustration, madness creates friction.
Caught in the madness of the moment, fear grips.
Unable to hear in the wind, madness strips.
Ears to the wind, we hear whispers that eclipse.

Listening intently, the wind whispers, love one another,
Hate and violence spilling over, no one gains, we hear.
From different paradigms, they come screaming.
Cease from madness for the sake of loving, we hear
The voice cries; stop and listen, stop the clanging.

The whispering voice cries; plead, respect, and tolerate.
Allow love to rule; treat others as you wish to be treated,
Respect and tolerate opposing ideas that debate.

Forcing ideological ideas only spurns futility.
Stop and listen, peaceably amid brutality.

Let peace come forth to stop the unrest.
Let love come forth to stop the hate.
Let sanity come forth to stop the madness.
Let wisdom come forth with respect that tolerates.
Let joy come forth to fill the heart with gladness.

~

May God's blessings be upon you as you go forth as a peacemaker planting seeds of the gospel of Jesus Christ everywhere you go.

Day 33

Our Eternal Home

John 14:1-2 *"Let not your heart be troubled; you believe in God, believe also in Me.* ^{2} *In My Father's House are many mansions, if it were not so, I would have told you.* **I go to prepare a place for you.**

Paul wrote to the Corinthian church in his first epistle, *"If Christ has not risen, your faith is futile; you are still in your sins. If only we have hope in Christ in this life, we are the most pitiable of all men."* Jesus rose from the dead to be the first fruits of all who follow Him. Before His death and resurrection, He left us with the promise of the eternal home He would be preparing for each of us who discover the path to the door.

God has put eternity in our hearts.[24] He's given us the Holy Spirit to reveal all that's in the Father's heart, which includes our heavenly home. Jesus gave us the gift of His Holy Spirit to know the things that have been freely given to us now and throughout eternity. The heavenly home He is preparing for us is full of treasures to discover throughout all eternity.

1 Corinthians 2:9-10 *But as it is written: "Eye has not seen, nor entered into the heart of man the things which God has prepared for those who love Him."* ^{10} *But God has revealed them to us through His Spirit. For His Spirit searches all things, yes, the deep things of God.*

Just think of some of the most extraordinary architectural talents that have gone into building some of the most magnificent homes you've ever seen. All those architectural gifts came from the greatest architect that ever lived, Jesus Christ.

Colossians 1:16 *For by Him all things were created in heaven and on earth, visible and invisible, whether thrones or dominions or principalities or powers. All things were created through Him and for Him.*

---

[24] Ecclesiastes 3:11

Our Eternal Home – Treasures from Above

The great Architect is building an eternal dwelling place designed specifically for us according to our hopes, desires, and longings. He is intimately acquainted with our ways and desires and knows precisely what's in our hearts even more than we do. The psalmist reminds us of how great God's thoughts are toward us when he says, *"How precious also are Your thoughts to me, O God!"*

God, the Father, wants nothing more than to give us the desires of our hearts as we delight in Him.[25] The dwelling place Jesus is preparing for us will fulfill all our spoken and unspoken desires. When we open the doors to our eternal dwelling places, our initial response will be extreme happiness, delight, and euphoria. There aren't enough words to describe the ecstasy and exuberance we will experience as we open the doors to these magnificent places Jesus is preparing for each of us who finds the path leading to the door.

Our responses to our eternal dwelling places will be beyond our comprehension, but when we walk through the doors, our initial reaction might be, "How did you know?" And His response might be, "How could I help but know! I'm the One who fearfully and wonderfully created and brought you forth. I saw your substance when it was yet unformed. I fashioned all your days when there was yet none of them. I comprehended all your paths and was acquainted with all your ways as you went on this great journey.[26] My eyes have constantly been watching over you in anticipation of this moment. How could I help but create something designed specifically for you and all you desire? Because of My great love for you, I could do nothing less. Welcome home! Enter into the joy of the Lord. Well done, good and faithful servant!"

John 14:6 Jesus said to him, "I am the way, the truth, and the life. No one comes to the Father except through Me.

Prayer

Father, thank you for all you do in me and for me, both in this life and the next.

---

[25] Psalm 37:4
[26] Psalm 139:3, 16-17, Matthew 25:23

Our Eternal Home – Treasures from Above

Poem: Homeward Bound

Marching forward towards the eternal city, we look.
Believing in Christ, He writes our names in His book.
Leaving temporary things behind, we press forward.
Looking for the city, whose maker is God, He rewards.
The Invisible kingdom in view, He transports.

Sacrificial Lamb given; the way is cleared to His throne.
In discovery, He shows the way to our eternal home.
Giving ourselves to His sacrifice, the path uncovers.
Belief in His Son, the gateway opens for exploration.
Homeward bound, beauty is seen of our eternal location.

Clothed in majesty, He comes to set up His throne.
With promises fulfilled, He prepares a place to be shown.
With eyes and ears seeing and hearing, beauty awaits.
According to our desires, the Great Architect mandates.
Clothed with new celestial bodies, we reign in the unknown.

The sting of death removed, we rejoice forevermore.
In healing waters, without pain or sorrow, we adore.
Bearing the image of the heavenly, He raises incorruptible.
In a moment, the eyes twinkle; we're changed, indestructible.
In His presence, joy is given with pleasures forevermore.

Reunited with those before us, we embrace and savor.
Hearts filled with wonder, we explore and discover.
In beauty prepared, discovery surpasses imagination.
Walking on streets of pure gold, we revel in celebration.
Inheritance fully divulged, we indulge, fully revealed.

Scriptures to Meditate Upon

1 Corinthians 15:14-19, Ecclesiastes 3:11, Psalm 34:7, Luke 11:9-13, 32:8, Matthew 6:4, Psalm 121:8, Matthew 25:16-23. Hebrews 6:19.

~

May the eternal blessing of God be with you in discovering all He has in store for you in this life and the one to come.

Day 34
The Suffering Messiah

Isaiah 7:14 *Therefore, the Lord Himself will give you a sign: Behold, the virgin shall conceive and bear a Son, and shall call His name Immanuel.*

Born of a virgin, He came to bring light to a world lost in darkness. With the legitimacy of His birth in doubt, many mocked and disbelieved. Many rejected Him for not having beauty, form, or comeliness to desire Him. Born of a hated minority, the Messiah proclaimed a kingdom with no end. Again, He was rejected, championing a cause so just and radical that it brought hate and jealousy from the traditional and established religious authorities.

Isaiah 53:3 *He is despised and rejected by men, a man of sorrows and acquainted with grief. And we hid, as it were, our faces from Him; He was despised, and we did not esteem Him.*

With the cards stacked against Him, He came as the Word made flesh in the glory of the only begotten of the Father, full of grace and truth. He came to His own, and His own did not receive Him.

Against all odds, He came to proclaim the coming of a new kingdom with power and authority, silencing those who stood against Him. Full of grace and mercy, He embraced those who were considered outcasts. He was a friend to sinners, tax collectors, prostitutes, lepers, the demon-possessed, and those needing healing. However, the religious leaders of the day shunned Him. As a man of sorrows and acquainted with grief, many hid their faces despising and not esteeming Him.

Amid rejection, He pressed forward in His Father's will and purpose with His face set like flint to those who embraced His ministry. Healing all who came to Him, He fulfilled the prophecy of Isaiah with the beating He received at the hands of those who mocked Him.

Enlisting a band of fishermen, misfits, and others, He went forth in the fullness of the Spirit, converting all those the Father drew with the love and power emanating from Him. They were transformed into disciples who went forth as He did, proclaiming, *"Not by might nor by power, but by His Spirit."*

After three and a half years of ministry, He was sold out and betrayed by one of His disciples as another denied Him. Like sheep led to slaughter, the religious leaders of the day stood by while crowning Him with a crown of thorns. Standing silently in their presence, they mocked and spat upon Him. If that was not enough, they beat Him beyond recognition. In their final humiliating act, they sentenced and crucified Him with common thieves. As He hung on the cross, those around Him continued to mock Him.

***Matthew 27:39-44** And those who passed by blasphemed Him, wagging their heads [40] and saying, "You who destroy the temple and build it in three days, save Yourself! If You are the Son of God, come down from the cross." [41] Likewise, the chief priests, also mocking with the scribes and elders, said, [42] "He saved others: Himself He cannot save. If He is the King of Israel, let Him now come down from the cross, and we will believe Him. [43] He trusted in God; Let Him deliver Him now if He will have Him, for He said, 'I am the Son of God.'" [44] Even the robbers who were crucified with Him reviled Him with the same thing.*

Jesus allowed Himself to be led like a sheep to the slaughter. He completely submitted His soul to the Father's will. Jesus knew full well every aspect of what was going to take place. He tried to explain to His disciples what would happen to Him in Jerusalem on more than one occasion, but they could not comprehend what He was saying. Finally, in the Garden of Gethsemane, the Father reminded Him of all that would occur. His prayer was, *"O My Father, if it is possible, let this cup pass from Me; nevertheless, not as I will, but as You will."* As the Scripture says, Jesus had to learn obedience through what He suffered, just as we do.

Jesus was able to submit to the process of obedience and the Father's will because He had the complete picture of what was to be accomplished by embracing His cross. As the book of Hebrews says, it was for the joy set before Him that He endured the cross, despising its shame.

Just as Jesus had to take up His cross to fulfill the Father's will, it is with us. We must embrace the cross and all it stands for to achieve the Father's will and purpose for our lives.

Matthew 10:38-39 *"And He who does not take up His cross and follow after Me is not worthy of Me. ³⁹ He who finds his life will lose it, and he who loses his life for My sake will find it.*

Just as Jesus needed a revelation of the Father's will for Him to embrace His cross, so it is with us. The Father has given us the Holy Spirit to search His heart on our behalves so that we might know His will and purpose for our lives. When we fill our hearts and minds with the revelation of the hope of our calling, it makes it much easier to embrace the cross while fellowshipping in the sufferings of Jesus.

Ephesians 1:17-20 *that the God of our Lord Jesus Christ, the Father of glory, may give you the spirit of wisdom and revelation in the knowledge of Him, ¹⁸ the eyes of your understanding being enlightened; that you may know what is the hope of His calling, what are the riches of the glory of His inheritance in the saints, ¹⁹ and what is the exceeding greatness of His power towards us who believe, according to the working of His mighty power ²⁰ which was worked in Christ when He raised Him from the dead and seated Him at His right hand in the heavenly places.*

Let each of us, for the joy set before us, willingly embrace the fellowship of His sufferings as we take up our crosses and follow Him. The rewards will be well worth it.

Prayer

Father, I thank You for all that You allowed Your only begotten Son to experience on my behalf. Help me take up my cross daily to be worthy of all He has accomplished on my behalf.

Poem: The Suffering Messiah

Born of a virgin, He came with doubt now shown.
Wrongly accused of illegitimacy, He came to His own.
Like a shining light, He came into the world, giving hope.

The Suffering Messiah – Treasures from Above

False expectations cast, He came fulfilling His Father's will.
Rejected and tested by religious leaders, He taught to fulfill.

By mighty healings and miracles, He enraged the wise.
Setting traps, they couldn't catch Him with their spies.
From kingdom perspectives, He spoke to those hearing.
Unprepared, many couldn't hear with hearts spearing.
In parables, He spoke to hearing hearts preparing.

Riding on a colt, they proclaimed Him the coming King.
Proclaiming a kingdom from another realm, He challenged.
With false expectations, they rejected Him as their King.
In deep sorrow, those closest to Him slept as He distressed.
Swords and clubs in an hour of darkness, they arrested.

Taken to authorities, falsely accused, disciples fled in fear.
A friend denying Him, looking on, He saw him so dear.
As a lamb led to slaughter, they prepared Him for sacrifice.
With a crown of thorns, a purple robe given, they mocked.
Sentenced to death, brutally beaten, they were shocked.

With our sins and grief bearing down, He hung on the cross.
Blood dripping, His Father looking away, He became sin for us.
Crying in agony, "Why have You forsaken Me?" He lost touch.
Giving up the ghost, beaten, chastised, and crucified, He died.
After three days freeing us from sin, He rose from the dead.

Scriptures to Meditate Upon

John 8:41-42, 8:48-52, 1:1-5, 14, Luke 17:20-21, Matthew 11:19, Isaiah 50:6-7, Luke 9: 51, Zechariah 4:6, Acts 1:8, Ephesians 1:17-22, John 19:1-6, Hebrews 5:8-9, 12:1-2, Isaiah 53:3-10.

~

May God richly bless you as you embrace the cross of Christ by partaking in the fellowship of His sufferings. As you partake of the same cup Jesus shared with His disciples, may you fulfill all He has planned for you.

Day 35
Standing Firm in Life's Storms

***Hebrews 12:27-28** Now this, "Yet once more," indicates the removal of those things that are being shaken, as of things that are made, that the things which cannot be shaken may remain. ²⁸ Therefore, since we are receiving a kingdom that cannot be shaken, let us have grace, by which we may serve God acceptably with reverence and godly fear.*

Today, many suffer from anxiety and a lack of peace while various storms blow across the world's landscapes. Storms such as disease, political unrest, terrorism, the constant threat of nuclear war, riots, homelessness, inflation, bigotry, drought, starvation, financial woes, health issues, natural disasters, and more threaten our peace of mind. However, during the storms of life, we have an anchor of hope that allows us to stand firm when turbulent winds blow. We are part of the kingdom that cannot be shaken.

***Hebrews 6:17-19** Thus God determining to show more abundantly to the heirs of promise the immutability of His counsel, confirmed it by an oath, ¹⁸ that by two immutable things, in which it is impossible for God to lie, we might have strong consolation, who have fled for refuge to lay hold of the hope set before us. ¹⁹* **This hope we have as an anchor to the soul, both sure and steadfast, and which enters the Presence behind the veil.**

For those dealing with fear, pain, depression, and anxiety, the worldly solution is to medicate them to numb what's happening. Once a year, I go to the VA Clinic for my annual checkup. They always ask me the same questions. What medications are you taking? Are you dealing with depression or anxiety? When I say to them, "I don't deal with depression, and I'm not taking medications," they look at me strangely and say, "Really!" They are so used to dealing with depression, anxiety, and medicating everyone; it surprises them when someone comes along who doesn't deal with depression or needs medicating. God has a better solution, although I understand some deal with clinical depression and need to be on medications. We have the ability in Christ to stand firm amid life's storms without being medicated. We can do all things through Christ, who strengthens us daily and always leads us in triumph. We have grace amid all that is shaking.

1 Thessalonians 5:23 *Now may the God of peace Himself sanctify you completely, and may your whole spirit, soul, and body be preserved blameless at the coming of our Lord Jesus Christ.*

God has designed our relationship with Him to keep our spirit, soul, and body healthy. Living according to God's designed ways will make us healthy in these three areas. God desires to show those of us who are the heirs of the promises that He is faithful in keeping His promises.

All the promises of God are yes and amen. God cannot lie. If He has promised us something in His word, we can stake our lives on it. His word says He has given us everything pertaining to life and godliness. This promise is part of the hope set before us, as the Scripture in the book of Hebrews implies. As we adjust and live according to what He's promised, we have peace of mind that frees us from anxious thoughts that give birth to depression. We can stand firm even when the circumstances of our lives may be saying something different. As we hold fast to our confession of hope, He is faithfully there to comfort and supply our needs.

Hebrews 10:23 *Let us hold fast the confession of hope without wavering, for He who promised is faithful.*

Aside from our hope in Christ and our inherited promises, Paul gives us a good prescription for standing firm and overcoming fear, anxiety, and depression in his letter to the Philippians.

Philippians 4:6-8 *Be anxious for nothing, but in everything by prayer and supplication, with thanksgiving, let your requests be made known to God;* ⁷ **and the peace of God, which surpasses all understanding, will guard your hearts and minds through Jesus Christ.** ⁸ *Finally, brethren, whatever things are true, whatever things are noble, whatever things are just, whatever things are pure, whatever things are lovely, whatever things* *are of good report. If there is any virtue and if there is anything praiseworthy—meditate on these things.*

Most of what Paul mentioned is the exact opposite of what is force-fed into our minds daily. We wonder why so many are dealing with depression and anxiety. If I filled my mind with what the world wants to force-feed me, I would probably be depressed, too. I purposely watch little news, especially local news, and refuse to fill my mind with all the political rhetoric from all spectrums and arguments. It is all so depressing. There is little that is of good report, trustworthy, and lovely that comes across the airwaves, yet that is what people fill their minds with daily. It takes discipline to resist the squeeze of the world, but if we want to stand firm during all that is going on today, we must follow Paul's advice to the Philippians and take the medicine he is prescribing.

Allow the anchor of hope to fill your minds and hearts with all the goodness God has to offer, and you will find yourself rejoicing in the Lord, standing firm in a sea of troubles without anxious thoughts. Allow treasures from above rather than the garbage spewed from the cesspools of the world to fill your hearts.

Prayer

Heavenly Father, help me fill my mind with those noble things of good report as I come to You with my prayers and supplications. Fill me with Your peace that surpasses all understanding. Help me meditate on all that's praiseworthy so I may stand firm during the storms that rage around me. Help me not get caught up in the whirlwinds of unbelief and worldly thinking with its rhetoric.

Poem: Standing Firm

In Your word, righteous ones are bold as a lion, You say!
Why are we sometimes in a place of weakness and prey?
Crying desperately, feeling trapped in hopelessness, we stray.
Where's life and victory, promised, looking for tomorrow?
Slipping into despair, we sometimes drown in sorrow.

Standing in our righteousness, we misstep and trip.
Fastening eyes on the surrounding hopelessness, we slip.
Not heeding love and freedom promised, we lose grip.
In disparity, all that's seen is pain, turmoil, hate, and wrath.
Was there a wrong turn taken somewhere missing the path?

Retracing steps, the path is found that was missed.
In Your word, light illuminates that which was dismissed.
What was not taken heed to that was ignored and resisted?
What was not applied that allowed slipping into despair?
Indeed, we find it when given to diligence and prayer.

Worthless things, selfish gain, and covetousness, that's it.
Turning towards You in all things, the soul refreshes.
Turning from worthless things, we stand firmly to attain.
Not envying prosperity with selfish ambition, we gain.
Turning to things above, the seed firmly plants.

In faithfulness and delighting in You, we're planted.
Committing and trusting, You bring to pass desires granted.
Taking heed, righteousness shines as a beacon of light.
As an abundance of peace fills, we stand, planted aright.
How was the path missed? Blinded by self-will, we lost sight.

Scriptures to Meditate Upon

2 Timothy 3:1-5, Matthew 24:4-13, 2 Corinthians 1:20, 2 Peter 1:2-3, 2 Timothy 2:13, 2 Corinthians 2:14, Philippians 4:13, Galatians 3:29.

~

May God richly bless you as you stand firmly on His promises with hope as the anchor of your soul.

Day 36
Embracing Your Future

When you think about your future, what do you sense? Do you feel hopeless when you think about your future, or is your heart filled with excitement? If you are walking in the Spirit and allowing the word of God to transform your thoughts, you will agree with God's thoughts for your life rather than allowing them to fill you with a sense of hopelessness. God's thoughts toward your future are full of peace and goodness. He desires to give you a future filled with hope.

***Jeremiah 29:11** For I know the thoughts that I think toward you says the Lord, thoughts of peace and not of evil, to give you a future and a hope.*

I often remind myself that God desires to give me a future filled with hope and vision. Whenever I lack faith in my future, I meditate on the above Scripture and others. Satan will do everything in his power to feed us negative thoughts regarding our future because he knows that when we bring our thoughts into the captivity of God's word and Spirit, he has no game. We can go forth in His will and purpose as overcomers, bringing his schemes and ploys to naught.

We all have a past filled with victories and failures. The enemy wants nothing more than to steal those victories by getting us to focus on our failures. It does not matter what happened in the past; every day in the Lord is new. His promise to us is to make all things new. No matter how discouraged or disillusioned you may have been in the past, the slate has been wiped clean. However, even though we are made new in God's eyes, it does not come automatically. We are encouraged in Scripture to gird up the loins of our minds and think differently about ourselves. As a man thinks, so is he. Our minds must be reprogrammed or renewed according to His Word and thoughts toward us.

Embracing Your Future – Treasures from Above

I Peter 1:13 *Therefore gird up the loins of your mind, be sober, and rest your hope fully upon the grace that is brought to you through the revelation of Jesus Christ.*

1 Peter 5:8 *Be sober, be vigilant; because your adversary, the devil, walks about like a roaring lion, seeking whom he may devour.*

As we give ourselves to His word and Spirit, they work together, transforming and conforming our minds to His thoughts and ways. As a result, we can face the future with faith and hope, knowing what He began in us will continue until our death or His second coming.

Philippians 1:6 *being confident of this very thing, that He who has begun a good work in you will complete it until the day of Jesus Christ.*

As we continually yield to the Holy Spirit and the word of God, they work together to build a future full of hope and confidence in bringing His goodness to pass, delighting our souls. His goodness includes everything given to us that pertains to life and godliness—a future filled with hope. Therefore, the apostle Paul said, *"To this end I also labor, striving according to His working, which works in me mightily."*

One of the things that can cause us to be depressed about our future is the fear of death. However, God has taken care of that as well. When God gave the apostle Paul a picture of eternity, his confession of faith became, *"To live is Christ, and to die is gain."*

Philippians 1:22-23 *For me to live is Christ, and to die is gain.* [22] *But if I live on in the flesh, this will mean the fruit of my labor; yet what I shall choose I cannot tell.* [23] *For I am hard-pressed between the two, having a desire to depart and be with Christ, which is far better.*

As we look to the future, God assures us that He removes the sting of death. As we meditate on what God prepared for us, He fills our hearts with joy and peace now and throughout eternity rather than foreboding. Nevertheless, death eventually comes to all of us, so we might as well prepare our hearts to accept it rather than fear it. As the writer of the book of Ecclesiastes wrote, *"The day of one's death is better than the day of one's birth."*

As we face the future with the hope set before us, it is crucial to consider how short our life here on earth is. Our life now is nothing more than a dress rehearsal for all eternity. Therefore, this is our opportunity to prepare ourselves as we metamorphose into our next life. James, the Lord's brother, gives us sound advice about spending time in this life.

***James 4:13-15** Come now, you who say," Today or tomorrow we will go to such a city, spend a year there, buy and sell, and make a profit;" [14] whereas you do not know what will happen tomorrow. For what is Your life?* **It is even a vapor that appears for a little time and then vanishes away.** [15] *Instead, you ought to say, "If the Lord wills, we will do this and that."*

In other words, James says that with our time in this life, we should dedicate ourselves to God's purposes. This dedication is what prepares us for eternal life in Jesus Christ.

Let me encourage you to align your thoughts about the future with the Father's will. When you do, you will have a future filled with hope and goodness. Let what is true breathe impetus into your spirit as your thoughts bring forth His captivity and limitless hope.

Prayer

Heavenly Father, I come to You today, asking forgiveness for not allowing Your thoughts about my future to fill my mind and heart. Help me have a heart of faith and belief that embraces Your goodness towards me. Fill my heart with assurance and confidence as I stare into my future. Thank you for the wonderful promises in Your word that breathe faith and assurance into my spirit.

Poem: Looking to the Future

Looking to the future, thoughts tend to drift into hopelessness.
Where are the thoughts once filling the mind with excitement?
In disparity; thoughts of fear, and uncertainty discourage.
With discouragement; disillusionment breaks into weariness.
Where are the dreams and desires once capturing the heart?

Looking to the future, we question, how has time vanished?
Can dreams and aspirations, once ruling the spirit, be revived?

Is it too late for His presence to burst forth with passion?
Will the future be filled with expectations of promises given?
Satan plundering, will Jesus give abundantly, filling the spirit?

Looking to the future, truth unfolding, God breathes impetus.
Gifts uncovered, life and hope burst forth with new seasons.
Thoughts brought into captivity, He gives eternal hope.
Looking to past victories, faith arises on the horizon.
Girding the loins of the mind, focus ignites determination.

Looking to the future, firmly planted, grace gives fresh starts.
Doubts and confusion washing away, fresh vision fills hearts.
Confidence embracing, new strength comes, now shown.
Joy flooding thirsty souls, hearts prepare for paths unknown.
Staring into the future, faith and hope replace uncertainty.

Scriptures to Meditate Upon

2 Corinthians 10:4-6, John 10:10, Revelation 12:10, 2 Corinthians 5:17, Proverbs 23:7, Romans 12:2, Colossians 1:29, Philippians 1:21-23, 1 Corinthians 15:55, Ecclesiastes 7:1.

~

May God's blessings and anointing be upon your life as you allow your thoughts to conform to His concerning your future. May you stare into your future with faith and confidence, knowing He who has begun a good work in you will continue it until the coming of Christ. God bless you!

Day 37
Grace Unlimited

John 1:14* And the Word became flesh and dwelt among us, and we beheld His glory, the glory as the only begotten of the Father, full of grace and truth.*

The greatest treasure from above the Father gave to the world was the gift of His only begotten Son, Jesus Christ, who came into the world as the Word made flesh, full of grace and truth.

When we believe in Jesus Christ as our resurrected Savior, we experience firsthand what it means to be saved by grace. Even though we did not deserve it, we realize God wiped the slate clean of our sins and shame. We now stand before our Judge innocent, without guilt. There no longer remains a reason to dull our senses with alcohol, drugs, or other things to cover our guilt and shame. We stand perfectly in the righteousness of Christ, our Savior, based on His performance rather than ours.

Because the Father has clothed us in the righteousness of Jesus, there's no reason to try and hide from God as Adam and Eve did when they sinned. Just as God covered them with the skin of an animal that had to have its blood shed, He covers us with the blood of His only begotten Son, the perfect Lamb of God, who has perfected those being sanctified forever. As a result, we can now come boldly into His presence at any time, knowing He is always there to revive us no matter what we may have done.

Leviticus 17:11* For the life of the flesh is in the blood, and I have given it to you upon the altar to make atonement for your souls, for it is the blood that makes atonement for the soul.*

Hebrews 10:14* For by one offering, He has perfected forever those who are being sanctified.*

As great and wonderful as our first taste of the unmerited favor is, there is much to experience as we explore the wonders of His grace. His grace and mercy are limitless in power and ability as they flow in and through us, connecting with every aspect of who the Father has created us to be.

The manifold grace of God is not something to take for granted. It will teach and bring us to the maturity the Father desires from all of us. It will equip us to reach beyond our carnal limitations and be the supernatural people He called us to be. With His divine nature taking root, we press forward to lay hold of all that Jesus Christ has freely given us, just as Peter urges us to do in his first epistle.

1 Peter 4:10-11 As each one has received a gift, minister it to one another, as good stewards of the manifold grace of God. ¹¹ As anyone speaks, let him speak as the oracles of God. **If anyone ministers, let him do it with the ability which God supplies,** *that in all things God may be glorified through Jesus Christ, to whom belong the glory and dominion forever and ever. Amen.*

God designed grace to lead and teach us as we go forward into all He planned for our lives. The Holy Spirit then comes commissioned by the Father to guide us inexorably into the conformity the Father has fashioned for us. The problem is we frustrate the process when we do not yield to His desires. His grace is designed to lead us away from our fleshly and sinful desires rather than giving in to them.

Titus 2:11-12 For the grace of God that brings salvation has appeared to all men, ¹² teaching us that denying ungodliness and worldly lusts, we should live soberly, righteously, and godly in this present age.

Until we receive the revelation of the multiplicity of God's grace toward us and how He wants to impart it in the form of divine abilities, we become stuck in cycles of sin, holding us back from being all He has ordained us to be.

It is when we take full advantage of all that His grace represents that we do not get caught up in playing games with God and frustrating His grace. As a result, the Holy Spirit does not get quenched from doing what the Father commissioned Him to do. Our part is to yield to Him in all things. Rather than using the grace of God to excuse our sins, we must allow it to teach us the importance of denying worldly lusts and ungodliness. As we do, we begin to experience His unlimited grace towards us. Because we have unlimited access to His grace, the Father fully expects us to embrace and use it for its intended value. It will transform our lives from mundane Christianity into mature sons and daughters of God as the Holy Spirit makes all grace abound toward us. As a result, God gives us abundant grace and sufficiency for every good work. It will be unlimited as He multiplies it unto us.

*2 Corinthians 9:8 And God is able to make **all grace abound** toward you, that you **always** having **all sufficiency in all things**, may have an abundance for every good work.*

Prayer

Heavenly Father, I come to You in humility with a desire to be used by You as Your grace freely pours into my life. Help me fully embrace Your divine abilities as they transform me into who You have called me to be.

Poem: Grace that Leads

Once bound in oppression, His grace, we taste so readily.
Freed from depression, His love, we sense so joyfully.
Filled with peace, in all joy, He leads to new domains.
Washed and made clean, grace takes hold in all foretold.
Without guilt or shame, we're free to soar in all told.

Freed from uncertainty and doubt, grace leads to new resolutions.
Freed from trouble and stress, grace leads to peaceful solutions.
Sowing seeds of faith, we press unchained and sustained in Him.
When temptations strike, grace teaches us to deny all ungodliness.
No longer bound by disobedience, we yield to the power of grace.

Given ways to escape, eyes wide open, the path ahead is shown.
Fleeing the old, grace freely given, we soar to the unknown.
No longer bound by carnal limitations, we yield to divine nature.
In all called to, there is nothing we can't do as grace exceeds.
In Christ, all things are done without difficulty as grace leads.

We give thanks to the One who gives His grace so freely.
Overcome by grace covering, we rejoice in His hovering.
Grace leading, He makes us conquerors in all endeavors.
Grace imparting, we soar easily as He leads triumphantly.
We give thanks to Him, who empowers so completely.

Scriptures to Meditate Upon

Ephesians 2:8-10, 2 Corinthians 5:21, Genesis 3:8, 1 John 1:9, 2:1-2, Genesis 3:21, John 1:29, Hebrews 4:24-16, Philippians 3:12-14, 2 Peter 1:2-3, Romans 6:1-2, 1 Thessalonians 5:19, 2 Corinthians 3:18, Romans 8:14.

~

May the favor of God be with you as you soar through all He has called you to do. May His Grace be limitless as you give yourself to His sufficiency in all things.

Day 38
Changing our Perspectives

Romans 12:2 *And do not be conformed to this world, but be transformed by the renewing of your mind, that you may prove what is that good and acceptable and perfect will of God.*

Our perspectives become a big part of our identity, shaping us as we grow and mature. When we come to Christ, everything changes. When the apostle Paul came to Christ, everything about him changed. Before coming to Christ, he was a zealot who stood with those who stoned Stephen to death, one of the first deacons of the early Church formed following the resurrection of Jesus Christ. Paul's perspectives in life caused him to put followers of Christ in prison while having others put to death for their testimony of Jesus Christ. After meeting Christ, he became one of the primary movers and shakers in the growth of the early Church. As one accused of turning the world upside down for Christ, he definitely changed his perspectives about life and religion.

As we move through life's stages, we encounter many ideas and opinions that form our perspectives on life and the world around us. Our parents, educators, churches, friends, workmates, political leaders, and others were all part of the parade of influencers who helped to form our belief systems. No matter what the source or sources that may have played a role in how our perspectives were shaped, for the most part, they were a mixture of half-truths and lies. As Jesus pointed out, Satan is the father of lies. John, the beloved disciple, said, *"The whole world lies in his lap."* Our perspectives and how we thought about everything mainly conformed to the world's thinking. Therefore, our thinking and views on life must change, as Paul encourages us in the opening passage above.

Our perspectives of life and the world around us need to change dramatically now that we have come to know Christ with a desire to be His disciples. Our minds and how we think about everything need to align with God's word and thoughts. Any change that comes about in our lives begins with how we think. The proverb says, *"As a man thinks, so is he."* As Dylan once wrote, *"Gonna Change My Way of Thinking,"* we must also change our thinking and perspectives of life according to God's thoughts and thinking.

Isaiah 55:8-9 *"For My thoughts are not your thoughts, nor are your ways, My ways," says the Lord.* ^{9} *"For as the heavens are higher than the earth, so are My ways, and thoughts than your thoughts."*

How do we bring thoughts and perspectives into agreement with God's thoughts that are so much higher and loftier than ours? There is an answer. Our Heavenly Father gave us two great resources to do this: the word of God and the Holy Spirit. As we balance these two sources working together, God can align our thoughts and ways with His.

Following His death, burial, and resurrection, when Jesus ascended into heaven, He poured the promise of the Holy Spirit out on all flesh to guide and instruct us in God's ways. His word was given to us by divine inspiration for the instruction of doctrine, reproof, and correction in righteousness.

Concerning the Holy Spirit, Jesus said, *"I still have many things to say to you, but you cannot bear them now. However, when He, the Spirit of truth, has come, He will guide you into all truth; for He will not speak on His own authority, but whatever He hears He will speak; and He will tell you things to come."*

Concerning the word of God, the writer of the book of Hebrews said, *"For the word of God is powerful, and sharper than any two-edged sword, piercing even to the division of soul and spirit, and of joints and marrow, and is a discerner of the thoughts and intents of the heart."*

We have excellent security with these two sources—the Word and Spirit. These two sources are our security because God designed them to work together, not apart. However, because God never imposes His will upon us, we must utilize them and ensure they work together.

Some Christians are more Spirit-oriented, while others are more word-inclined. When a person is more Word-inclined and not dependent upon the Spirit's input, they become somewhat legalistic and out of balance. On the other hand, when one becomes more reliant upon the Holy Spirit and does not heed God's Holy written word, they become out of balance with too much wildfire. Therefore, we must honor both sources equally to fully experience coming into alignment with God's thoughts and ways.

The Word of God should always have precedence over the Holy Spirit's influence when there is perceived conflict between the two sources. The reason for this is quite simple. When the Spirit's revelation enters our spirit, it is first pure and unadulterated. It then must pass through the doorways of our minds, still undergoing the sanctifying process. What we hear must be submitted to the purity of God's word to remain pure. Without God's word as a filter, His revelation is distilled through our un-sanctified thoughts and emotions, distorting the truth.

When Peter compared his experience of hearing the voice of God to the written word of God, He said, *"We also have a more sure word of prophecy,"* speaking of the prophetic word that came by holy men of God who spoke as the Holy Spirit moved them. The following Scriptures show that we need both sources to teach and instruct us.

Psalm 12:6 *The words of the Lord are pure words, like silver, tried in a furnace of earth, purified seven times.*

1 John 2:20, 27 *But you have an anointing from the Holy One, and you know all things.* ^{27} *But the anointing which you have received from Him abides in you, and you do not need that anyone teach you; but as the same anointing teaches you concerning all things, and is true, and is not a lie, and just as it has taught you, you will abide in Him.*

As we give ourselves to the study of God's Word and allow the Holy Spirit to have free reign in our lives, we will remain balanced Christians. We will have immersed ourselves in Him, with His thoughts and ways transforming our perspectives.

Changing our Perspectives – Treasures from Above

Prayer

Heavenly Father, I submit my mind, heart, and attitudes to You so my thoughts and ways are filled with Your perspectives that will transform me into the person You have created me to be.

Poem: Transforming Perspectives

Weakened by life's circumstances, we cry in desperation.
Broken and shattered without hope, we cry in frustration.
Caught in webs of self-pity, we complain, giving into strife.
Where does help come from? We cry out in exasperation.
Where are Your promises of all things pertaining unto life?

Perspectives transforming, strength pours through.
Fresh wind filling, He gives sail as His Spirit renews.
In obedience to His word and Spirit, transformation molds.
Mounting on wings of an eagle, divine abilities take hold.
Weariness once gripping, desperation turns into gold.

His wind taking us to places unknown, faith erupts.
Seeing beyond circumstances, courage interrupts.
From a distance, the father's blessings are visualized.
With abundance in view, zeal within rushes forward.
Taking pleasure in Him, we no longer cry to be heard.

With promises taking root, we give thanks to Him alone.
Trusting, we learn peace and contentment, now grown.
Strengthened in His presence embraced, we move forward.
Sufficiency of grace in all circumstances, we lean into Him.
Powered by Word and Spirit, we press, filled to the brim.

Scriptures to Meditate Upon

2 Corinthians 5:17, Acts 7:57, Acts 8:1-3, 17:6, John 8:44, 1 John 5:19, Proverbs 23:7, 2 Timothy 3:16-17, Hebrews 4:12, 2 Peter 1:16-21.

~

May God bless you richly as you walk in the Father's ways and thoughts.

Day 39
Embracing the Fear of God

Proverbs 9:10 *The fear of the Lord is the beginning of wisdom, and the knowledge of the Holy One is understanding.*

If we are to be wise in the ways of God, it begins by embracing the fear of the Lord. In the above Scripture, the writer directly correlates the fear of the Lord and the knowledge of the Holy, which brings understanding. God has designed the fear of the Lord to bring us into deeper realms of intimacy with our Lord and Savior. Without the intimacy of fearing God, we will not know the Lord in the way He desires for us.

There is much to say concerning the fear of the Lord throughout the Bible. Moses said God requires us to fear Him and walk in His ways. David said God is to be greatly feared in the congregation of His saints. Solomon said that man's whole duty is to fear God and keep His commandments. Isaiah said we must sanctify the Lord and let Him be our fear. Jesus said to fear Him, who can destroy our souls in Hell. Paul said we are to work out our salvation in fear and trembling. Peter said we are to pass our time of sojourning in fear. The writer of the Book of Hebrews said it is a fearful thing to fall into the hands of a living God.

As mentioned, the fear of God is the beginning of wisdom, but what does that involve? To begin with, it is tremendous respect and awe for who God is in His sovereignty, majesty, and power. However, it also entails much more as we consider how it affects our walk with Him. Therefore, we must embrace it with our hearts, minds, and souls as we seek to be who God called us to be.

In today's Christian culture, the fear of God is often watered down when it comes to trembling in His presence. It settles for a sense of awe and respect, but the fear of God goes beyond that. We must embrace His severe side and tremble before God, who can cast our souls into hell for eternity. Passages from the books of Hebrews and Philippians bear this thought out in the following passages.

Hebrews 12:28-29 *Therefore, since we are receiving a kingdom which cannot be shaken, let us have grace, by which we may serve God acceptably with reverence and godly fear. ^{29} For our God is a consuming fire.*

Philippians 2:12b-13 *But now much more in my absence, work out your own salvation with fear and trembling; ^{13} for it is God who works in you both to will and do for it is His good pleasure.*

We are urged to tremble at God's word, which means having a high regard for it. Only as we take time to read and commit to the truths contained therein will we experience more of an intimate understanding of who God is and what He desires from us.

The amazing thing from the above passage is that God works in us to change our will to embrace Him in fear and trembling. As God works this change in us, it helps us connect to His sovereign purposes. It is through the fear of God that His sovereignty converges with our free will to get the job done.

God is always watching, even when we do not sense His presence. He continually examines every thought and motive, including our words and actions, as they pass before Him. When we are constantly aware of His ongoing presence, we're more careful with our secret thoughts, words, and actions, knowing that everything eventually comes to light. We must take all of this into account as we sojourn in fear.

Proverbs 5:21 *(NIV) For your ways are in full view of the Lord, and he examines all your paths.*

Fearing God embraces His hatred of sin, as shown throughout the Old and New Testaments. He sees sin and evil going against the grain of all He has destined for those who follow Him. God considers the destruction it causes, which triggers the breakdown of cultures, resulting in the decay of all He created. Therefore, He expects us to hate sin and evil as He does.

Proverbs 8:13 *The fear of the Lord is to hate evil, pride and arrogance and the evil way.*

Fearing God also embraces His discipline. Once we experience salvation and are born again, it does not take long to realize we still have foolish and sinful ways that God must deal with. God has ways of dealing with them through His discipline by bringing these areas to the front and center.

Hebrews 12:5-7 *And have you forgotten the exhortation which speaks to you as sons: My son do not despise the chastening of the Lord, nor be discouraged when you are rebuked by Him;* [6] *for whom the Lord loves, He chastens, and scourges every son whom He receives.* [7] *If you endure chastening, God deals with you as sons; for what son is there whom a father does not chasten?*

Fearing God will also embrace the fear of Hell and the Lake of Fire. There is much to say in the Old and New Testaments concerning Hell and the Lake of Fire. The Bible teaches that life continues after the physical death of the body. God created man with a natural, physical body and an eternal soul. The soul of man consists of who we are. It is the center of our mind, will, and emotions. The Bible teaches that life is eternal. Because the soul is immortal, we will spend eternity in Heaven or Hell.

Daniel 12:2 *And many of those who sleep in the dust of the earth shall awake, some to everlasting life, some to shame and everlasting contempt.*

As we are faithful to observe everything regarding what it means to fear God, He will prepare as useful vessels who bring glory and honor to our Lord and Savior, the Lord Jesus Christ.

Psalm 107:43 *Whoever is wise will observe these things, and they will understand the lovingkindness of the Lord.*

Prayer

Heavenly Father, help me to embrace every aspect of who you are. Teach me to tremble at Your word with the highest respect and regard so I may fully understand Your lovingkindness as You wash me in Your love.

Poe: The Necessity of Fear the Lord

Coming to the Father, we stand in awe of all He is.
To those passing by, He is to be feared and revered.
His goodness and severity, we learn from Him.
Trembling at His word, wisdom is imparted.
In the congregation of the saints, He is to be feared.

As Moses said, we must fear God and walk in His ways.
As Isaiah said, we are to let Him be our fear.
As Jesus said, fear Him, who can destroy your soul in Hell.
As Peter said, pass the time of sojourning in fear.
It's a fearful thing to fall into the hands of a living God.

In the fear God, perfect love casts out all fear.
Trembling at His Word, He blesses beyond measure.
Working out salvation in fear and trembling, He works.
In His severity, He is perfectly righteous in all His ways.
Examining us, our ways are in full view of Him.

Standing before Him, we embrace His discipline.
With every secret thought, we know He's watching.
Standing in righteousness, we hate sin and evil.
In fear, we recognize the reality of Hell.
In fear, we understand He disowns those who disown.

To those who fear Him, His lovingkindness is understood.
To those who fear Him, Angels encamp around them.
To those who fear Him, He preserves them from corruption.
To those who fear Him, His intimacy is enjoyed.
To those who fear Him, He restores and sets free.

Scriptures to Meditate Upon

Deuteronomy 10:12, Psalm 89:7, Ecclesiastes 12:13, Isaiah 8:13, Matthew 10:28, 1 Peter 1:17, Hebrews 10:31.

~

May the blessing of God be upon you as you embrace His goodness and severity. May you experience all His blessings as He loads you daily with His benefits.

Day 40
Trusting in God Alone

Proverbs 3:5-6 *Trust in the Lord with all your heart and lean not on your own understanding; ⁶ in all your ways acknowledge Him, and He shall direct your paths.*

Psalm 37:5 *Commit your way to the Lord, trust also in Him, and He shall bring it to pass.*

Trusting in God alone is where the rubber hits the road. Our belief in God and His Son, Jesus Christ, gives birth to our faith, but trust in Him alone allows us to experience the reality of our belief and faith. Without trust, we will never experience the joys of His everlasting love toward us. As we trust Him with our lives, He leaves a deposit of Himself with His treasures from above flowing in and through us.

As we enter this newfound faith, we discover God gave us everything we need concerning our lives through His Word. Are we trusting in God alone to meet our needs, or are we leaning on our understanding to get what we need? Do we trust in God by acknowledging Him in all our ways, or do we carry on like He doesn't exist? As the writer of the book of Hebrews says, *"For He who comes to God must believe that He is and that He is the rewarder of those who diligently seek Him."* The above word from the book of Hebrews is a powerful Scripture, but it must be conveyed into trust for its truth to become a reality. Both Solomon and David point us toward this truth in the above verses.

The more we put our trust in God alone, the more we experience all He desires to pour into our lives from His eternal treasures. However, sometimes, God pours into our lives out of His abundance despite our lack of faith and trust to give us a sample or a mustard seed of what He has to offer. This mustard seed of faith must be nurtured with trust as we go from faith to faith. It takes a solid commitment to God and His ways to maintain the kind of trust that brings to pass all that He desires to do in our lives. Faith without works is dead. When we learn to trust God in the simple things we encounter daily, the significant storms of life that hit us have little effect. Because of our trust and reliance upon Him, we build a reservoir of faith, ready to trust God no matter the circumstances or how severe the storms of life may be. As we continually sow seeds of faith in all we experience, He gives abundant grace and mercy in times of great need. It is the law of sowing and reaping as it applies to our faith and trust in God.

2 Corinthians 9:8-11 And God is able to make all grace abound toward you, that you, always having all sufficiency in all things, may have an abundance for every good work. [9] As it is written: "He has dispersed abroad, He has given to the poor; His righteousness endures forever." [10] Now may He who supplies seed to the sower, and bread for food, supply and multiply the seed you have sown and increase the fruits of your righteousness, [11] while you are enriched in everything for all liberality, which causes thanksgiving through us to God.

Let the above Scripture encourage you to commit all your ways unto Him by acknowledging God in everything you do. As a result, you will grow from faith to faith by trusting in Him while encountering various trials and hardships.

Prayer

Heavenly Father, help me trust You for every aspect of my life. I commit my way to You today to guide and direct me as I acknowledge all my ways before You. Make my life a blessing to all those I meet.

Devotional Poem: In You Alone

In You alone, trusting, we lean upon Your word and Spirit.
With Your word a lamp unto the path, we look to You alone.
You alone are the One giving direction to the weary ones.
Waiting upon You alone, daily, we drink from Your Spirit.
With Your word washing over the mind, it renews daily.

In You alone, we rely upon, giving breath to revive.
Casting all cares and burdens upon You, You relieve.
Waiting, divine ability flows through as we believe.
In You alone, the weary mount on the wings of an eagle.
Seated in heavenly places, our spirits soar with You.

Your Spirit and word fill the mind with thoughts, so fine.
With the mind of Christ, forward we go into all that's divine.
With all things given concerning life and godliness, we dine.
Taking possession of Your divine nature, we press forward.
In You alone, to the upward call and prize, we press onward.

With Your precious promises, we escape to You alone.
With the world's corruption no longer holding back, we soar.
We adore You alone, forever walking together in Your love.
Now made complete and whole, Your love washes over.
Forever grateful, standing in Your presence, righteous we are.

Scriptures to Meditate Upon

Proverbs 3:5-6, Psalm 119:105, 1 Corinthians 12:13, Ephesians 5:25, 1 Peter 5:7, 2 Corinthians 9:8, Isaiah 40:31. Ephesians 2:6, Philippians 3:14, Peter 1:3-4, Hebrews 10:14, 2 Corinthians 5:21.

May the blessing of God be upon you as you learn to trust Him in all things, even the most minute circumstances you encounter daily.

About the Author

Ken Birks is an ordained Pastor/Teacher in the Body of Christ. For the past twenty years, he has served as an elder, staff pastor, and Bible teacher at The Rock of Roseville in California. He is semi-retired with a writing ministry and serves as a wedding officiant in the Sacramento region. Prior to this, Ken was the Senior Pastor of Golden Valley Christian Center, a Spirit-filled, non-denominational church in Roseville, for twelve years.

Ken attended and graduated from the Charismatic Bible College of Anchorage, where he entered a relationship with Apostle Dick Benjamin, who was then the Sr. Pastor of Abbott Loop Christian Center (ALCC) in Anchorage, Alaska.

Aside from The Lord Jesus Christ, the core of Ken's spiritual being and the person he's become directly results from the influence and teaching he received from Dick Benjamin for more than 25 years." Other influences have been Bob Mumford from Life Changers and, in the past 18 years, Pastor Francis Anfuso of The Rock of Roseville.

Ken has been married to Lydia for 45 years plus. They have two adult children and consider them their highest calling, along with the many teens and children they have been foster or surrogate parents to over the past 25 years.

Ken also has an internet ministry called "Sowing Seeds of Faith" at kenbirks.com. Sowing Seeds of Faith reaches over 4,500 unique visitors a month with free Bible studies, devotional poetry, sermon outlines, video messages, and other Bible study materials to help equip saints for the work of the ministry.

Books and Workbooks by Ken Birks

Prophetic Purposes and the Zeal of the Lord

Do you believe worldwide revival is possible? Try to imagine what it will be like when the Church rises in the glory spoken of by Isaiah, the prophet. Just as God, in His sovereignty, brought forth the Messiah according to the timing of Daniel's prophecy, He will bring forth the prophetic purpose of a worldwide revival according to His timing. God's people, who He plants in every city, village, town, and countryside worldwide, will stand up as the vast army, just as Ezekiel prophesied. God will fulfill His prophetic and sovereign purposes. As God breathes on the dry bones prophesied by the prophet Ezekiel, His glory will fill all in all, just as Paul prophesied to the Ephesians. This book explores and instructs how to be ready for this prophecy and others that He will fulfill before the coming of Christ to set up His eternal kingdom on earth as it is in heaven.

The Adventures of Space and Hobo

The Adventures of Space and Hobo tells the story of Ken's nomadic life after Vietnam. It explores the on-the-ground confusion and chaos of the Vietnam War and its effects on a generation and those who served. Named "Space" by a new friend, Hobo, Ken, and his traveling companion hit the road to partake of all the possibilities of that generation in search of adventure and uncharted experiences. The story takes us step by step along the path of awakening a lost

Books and Workbooks by Ken Birks

soul on his way to understanding himself, his path, and the meaning of his life.

The Journey
Discovering the Invisible Path

The Journey gives you a glimpse into God's path for your life. Whether you just started your journey anywhere in the middle or you're detoured and lost your way, this practical guidebook will shine the light on the invisible path. This hidden path leads to God's goodness and experiencing His kingdom within and to the most incredible adventure of your life.

Francis Anfuso says, "Ken makes complex concepts simple and masterfully unpacks the Bible's greatest mysteries. He provides a sure foundation to build a lifetime of insight."

The Rise of the Anointed Ones

Ken Birks has written a masterpiece of superb continuity. Each devotional stands on its own, but together, they propel you into a rewarding journey of experiencing God's presence in tumultuous times. The majestic flow from theme to theme contains powerful prophetic revelation as God calls His end-time warriors to arise. The poems that follow each devotional are Davidic and musical. This book is like a voice in the wilderness calling God's beloved away from all that distracts Him who is jealous for His bride. – *Ed Becker and David Fredrickson.*

For more information on these books and other materials by Ken Birks, please visit www.booksbyken.com.

Books and Workbooks by Ken Birks

Treasures of the Heart
Prose and Poetry Refreshing the Soul

As you read through the devotional prose and poetry found in this book, you will find a beautiful blend of timeless truths fitly applied to today's culture and challenges that fill your heart with treasures from above. The Heavenly insights will challenge you to grow in the knowledge of the Son of God.

The majestic flow from one poem to the next contains powerful prophetic wisdom and revelation that will fill your hearts and minds.

Biblical Perspectives Course

This course features lessons designed to give you a solid Biblical foundation in the elementary truths of God's Word. The lessons have three things in mind—building a doctrinal foundation, developing godly character, and helping you discover and find God's destiny and purpose for your life. Please see the following website for more information and Lesson Titles:

More Biblical Perspectives Course

This course features lessons focused on three major areas of our Christian growth - doctrine, character, and destiny.

These lessons were designed to give you the Biblical understanding to strengthen your Christian foundation and take you on a deeper walk with God.

Please see the following website for more information and lesson titles:

www.kenbirks.com/perspectives-both/

References and Reviews

Dr. Jay Zinn
Founder and Author of The Discipleship Group, a national and international program for developing and equipping disciples to become disciple-makers.

Few authors can take theology and turn it into a devotional series of divine, inspiring nuggets and poetry. Ken Birks is an author who penetrates your heart and soul to know God better. I highly recommend his 40-Day Devotional book—Treasures From Above. — Dr. Jay Zinn.

Jim Feeney
Ph.D., Former Sr. Pastor and "Owner and Webmaster at Pentecostal Bible Studies and Free Pentecostal Sermon Central"

I've known Pastor Ken Birks for several decades. He and I have worked in various ministerial capacities in the same family of churches. Ken is held in extremely high esteem among our many pastoral colleagues. He is a minister with a firm grasp of the Word of God, a wide variety of administrative skills, a heart for souls, a proven experiential familiarity with the gifts of the Holy Spirit, and an unwavering commitment to the work of the Lord.

John Dubler
Senior Pastor of Good Shepherd Bible Chapel

Ken Birks is a highly effective teacher of the Scriptures. He combines a healthy respect for the Word with enthusiasm and personal experiences that match his teaching. Ken is a man of unimpeachable integrity, and his longevity in the Body of Christ as a pastor gives credence to the message of hope and encouragement that he brings to all.

References and Reviews

Phoenix Larsen
Poet/Writer

I have never met anyone with the holistic view of scripture that Ken has. As an avid devotional reader, I have never read one that ties scripture and poetry into daily readings to make something beautiful. I liken his poetry to Robert Frost, who can take everyday circumstances and translate them into something transcendent. Ken has the talent to interpret God's word understandably but preserves the complexity of truth. Often, it is hard for me to transform scripture into prayer, but the daily prayers within truly help me connect the dots. He sincerely walks in the truth he teaches. I recommend this for anyone who wants to see God's word from multiple angles of teaching and poetry.

Doug Hartline
Retired Information Technology Director

When thinking about reading a devotional, one must ask oneself two questions – is it relevant, and what makes it stand apart from the myriad of devotionals one can choose from? From my perspective, devotionals can be vital tools to improve our quiet time experience with God. They should be able to bring scriptural insight to us. Scripture is far more important than the words of even the most famous of authors, for it is Scripture that penetrates our souls with God's wisdom and daily guidance.

It is incredible prose and poetry, however, that separates Ken's devotional books and makes them stand out. Poetry can shine a light on God's Word from a different angle in a way that helps us look at it much deeper and often more profoundly. It gives us a unique ability to understand and appreciate God's Word in ways we may never have thought of before. We are suddenly confronted with beauty and clarity in our perceptions of our world and God's Kingdom.

Online Connections

www.kenbirks.com
Sowing Seeds of Faith, Bible Studies and More

www.kenbirks.com/videos
Video Sermons by Ken Birks

www.straitarrow.net
Bible Studies, Seminars, and More

www.straitarrow.net/devotional-poetry
Biblical Devotional Poetry

www.straitarrow.net/Newsletters
Bi-Monthly Newsletters

www.booksbyken.com
How to order Ken's books and materials.

www.sacramento-wedding-officiants.com
Wedding Officiating.

Email: klbirks@gmail.com

X Formally Twitter: @klbirks

Linkedin: www.linkedin.com/in/kenbirks

www.ingramcontent.com/pod-product-compliance
Lightning Source LLC
Chambersburg PA
CBHW050319120526
44592CB00014B/1973